★ ★ ★ ★ ★ ★ ★ ★ ★ ★ ★ ★

FLASHBACK

Other Books by C. R. Roseberry

Capitol Story
The Challenging Skies
Steamboats and Steamboat Men
A History of the New York State Library
From Niagara to Montauk: The Scenic Pleasures of New York State
Glenn Curtiss: Pioneer of Flight
Albany: Three Centuries a County

Also Available through Washington Park Press Ltd.

In and Around Albany
by Susanne Dumbleton and Anne Older, 1980

O Albany!
by William Kennedy (co-published with Viking Penguin Inc.)

Ireland
by William Dumbleton (in cooperation with SUNY Press)

In and Around Albany, Schenectady & Troy
by Susanne Dumbleton and Anne Older, 1985

★ ★ ★ ★ ★ ★ ★ ★ ★ ★ ★ ★

FLASHBACK

A FRESH LOOK AT ALBANY'S PAST

C. R. ROSEBERRY

Edited by
Susanne Dumbleton

Washington Park Press Ltd.
Albany, New York

Copyright © 1986 by Washington Park Press Ltd. All rights reserved. Printed in the United States of America. No part of this book may be used or reproduced without written permission except in the case of brief quotations embodied in critical articles or reviews. Information is available through

Washington Park Press Ltd.
7 Englewood Place
Albany, New York 12203
(518) 465-0169

Library of Congress Cataloging in Publication Data

Roseberry, Cecil R.
   Flashback, a fresh look at Albany's past.

   Bibliography: p. 179.
   Includes index.
   1. Albany (N.Y.)—History. 2. Albany Region (N.Y.)—History. I. Dumbleton, Susanne. II. Title.
F129.A357R67   1986   974.7'43   86-24651
ISBN 0-9605460-4-9

Acknowledgment is made to the publishers of Capital Newspapers for permission to reprint portions of articles which appeared in the *Times Union*. "Glenn H. Curtiss," originally appeared in *Glenn Curtiss: Pioneer of Flight*, published by Doubleday & Company, Inc.

FOR MARY

Contents

Introduction *1*

PART ONE: EPISODES
1614 Enter the Europeans *5*
1690 Massacre at Schenectady *9*
1754 The Fear of Attack *14*
1804 The Infamous Duel *20*
1860 Hopes Dashed *31*
1861 The Gun-Toting Mayor *37*
1861 Lincoln and Booth *43*
1862 The Race for the Monitor *52*
1865 Booth's Bullet *60*

PART TWO: SET CHANGES
Downtown Albany *75*
North Albany *84*
The South End *92*
Capitol Hill *100*
Washington Park *110*
West Albany *116*
Westland Hills and Pine Hills *120*
The Pine Bush *125*

PART THREE: SUPPORTING PLAYERS
Hudson and Champlain *133*
The Patroons *140*
Sir William Johnson *145*
Martin Van Buren *150*
Chester A. Arthur *156*
William F. (Billy) Barnes *162*
Glenn H. Curtiss *166*

PART FOUR: BIBLIOGRAPHIES
Books *179*
Chronological Listing of Selected Articles and Books *179*
Thematic Listing of Selected Articles and Books *184*
Index *193*

Tip Roseberry tracks down a story at Tanglewood in the '50s.

Introduction

IN 1979, WHILE DOING RESEARCH for various Washington Park Press publications, I would stumble upon stories by C. R. (Tip) Roseberry. The word "stumble" here is appropriate, for Mr. Roseberry's *Times Union* articles were available only in scattered clippings, mostly undated and all in an advanced state of decay—their edges crumbling, the ink long since rubbed from the many folds, and the type barely distinguishable from the deepening brown of the news-sheet. The condition of the clippings was the least of the barriers, however. Access was the chief problem: *Capital Newspapers* are not indexed, the vertical file at the Albany Public Library has no cross-referencing system, and the typescripts of the original drafts, which Mr. Roseberry had donated to the McKinney Library of the Albany Institute of History and Art, had been dispersed throughout the Institute collection.

My growing sense of the value of this neglected and deteriorating material was certified by William Kennedy in *O Albany!* "His stories in the *Times Union,* covering so many facets of the city, are an invaluable record of history to which attention should be paid. He should be collected. His articles should also be made the subject of a bibliography as soon as possible to make life easier for people like me who look things up as a way of life."

In 1985, supported by a sabbatical leave from Albany College of Pharmacy, I undertook a search for Mr. Roseberry's work, with an eye to publishing selected pieces and making others more readily available through a bibliography. Mr. Roseberry cooperated fully and the job grew as we decided not merely to reprint but rather to rewrite, update, expand, and combine. It grew further when we chose to include material from his books and other publications. The results of our efforts are here in the text of this book and the bibliographies.

In our selection we focused on cogent material which is currently difficult for the general public to unearth. We worked on each piece individually, finetuning prose, eliminating repetition, and adding details. As we stood back from our work, we realized that we had created a book which portrayed a city enlivened by high drama—complete with startling set changes, remarkable coincidences, and players fit for the operatic stage. It had become a collection of flashbacks—sharp insightful penetrations into the city's past which served to illuminate the present.

We do believe that the assembled pieces, leaping and lingering as they do through the different eras in the life of the city, give a sense of what life was like over the centuries, for the powerful as well as the unheralded, the privileged as well as the despised. We believe one also comes away with a clear understanding of why and how Albany became what it is—a metropolis with a keen sense of itself as both a distinctive entity and an integral part of the human continuum.

Susanne Dumbleton

PART ONE

★ ★ ★ ★ ★ ★ ★ ★ ★ ★ ★ ★ ★

Episodes

1614

★ ★ ★ ★ ★ ★ ★ ★ ★ ★ ★ ★ ★ ★

Enter the Europeans

THE WHOLE THING STARTED because there happened to be, in the prospering cities of western Europe, a lively market for the pelts of forest animals. Furs were status symbols nearly as prized as precious stones. Monarchs strutted in ermine, while nobles, clergy, and wealthy merchants lined and trimmed their garments with the softest fur.

To supply this demand, a small trading post—fortified and encircled by a moat—was opened for business with the Indians in 1614 on Castle Island (Kasteel Eylandt, as the Dutch spoke), in the Hudson River where the Normanskill flows down. It was named Fort Nassau, to honor Prince Maurice of Orange and Nassau, admiral general of Netherlands armies during their successful fight for liberation from Spanish tyranny.

Fort Nassau was the seed from which the city of Albany grew. In place before any fort or enduring settlement on Manhattan Island, it was the first established center of trade in the colony. Castle Island, with the passage of time, became Van Rensselaer Island, then Westerlo Island. In the end it ceased to be an island at all, joined to the mainland by fill in the Island Creek.

While Fort Nassau remained, this minuscule island was an important spot in the known world. It was well marked on the best map of America then charted. Financiers, merchants, mariners, and the crowned sovereigns of Europe perused this map, noting well the location of Castle Island.

When the fort was built, Shakespeare was living at Stratford on the fruits of his scrivening, and his plays were being regularly produced at the Globe. Francis Bacon was writing his essays. Queen Elizabeth was ten years dead, succeeded by her cousin, James I, who had ordered a fresh translation of the Bible. The settlers at Jamestown (named for him) were struggling for survival. The *Mayflower* was still in England, not to set sail for another six years. Spain, to the envy of rival nations, was raking in gold and silver from her ruthless American conquests. This precious metal was reinforcing Spain's position as the financial capital of all Europe, stimulating investment in further exploration to stake out yet more riches.

It is not known if the Dutch were the first European settlers on Castle Island. Circumstantial evidence suggests that they were not. The Indians who visited Henry Hudson's vessel were savvy enough to bring furs with them; they already knew what white men wanted. On Adriaen Block's famous "Figurative Map" of 1614 is the notation, "But as far as one can understand from what the Maquaas [Mohawks] say and show, the French came with sloops as high up as their country to trade with them." Many years later a Dutchman wrote of visiting Castle Island and seeing earthen mounds, not the ruins of Fort Nassau; he said he was told the Spaniards had built a fort there, though he doubted if they were Spaniards.

What is certain is that fur trade with American aborigines had been going on along the coast for many years before the Dutch arrived, that American furs were making an impact on the European market, and that France was profiting thereby.

Out from under the despotic rule of Spain at last, with a 12-year truce, and established as a republic of United Provinces with a zeal for civil and religious liberties, the Netherlands bestirred itself. The Dutch, born mariners and shrewd merchants, were already engaged in some trade with the East Indies. Because it was a long way around the Cape of Good Hope, the Dutch, like others, sought a shorter route to the Orient. The idea of a Northeast Passage—up around Norway and the Arctic coast of Russia—seemed the most logical.

The fashion of fur-wearing, begun during the Middle Ages, had depleted the fur animals of western Europe. Dutch traders had been importing furs from Russia at stiff prices. When the flood of high quality, cheaper furs came from Canada, the Dutch could not meet the competition. They, too, craved an American source.

The French had staked their claim to Canada. The English dominated Virginia and had laid claim to all the coast from Spanish Florida to New France, but as yet had no settlement north of Jamestown.

This was how matters stood when the hired navigator, Captain Henry Hudson, sailed back with his disappointing tiding that the river he had ascended was not a Northwest Passage to Cathay. But the report he forwarded to Amsterdam held another item that made the Dutch merchants prick up their ears: the natives who boarded his ship had brought fine beaver and otter skins for bartering.

What went on during the four years between Hudson's return and the planting of Fort Nassau is vague. It is certain, however, that there was quite a bit of trans-Atlantic activity on the part of the Dutch to cash in on Hudson's discovery.

Promptly in 1610, some Amsterdam merchants sent out another ship under command of Hudson's mate, Hudson himself having been compelled to return to British service. For some reason, this vessel failed to relocate the river, as did the next. Their navigation must have been poor.

Meanwhile, Captain Hendrick Christiaensen, on a return voyage from the West Indies, swung up the coast and located New York Harbor. Back in Holland, he teamed up with Captain Adriaen Block to take a better look at the mouth of the river and its environs. How far upstream they came that time does not appear. But they either captured or persuaded two young Indians—sons of chiefs, it was said—to return to Holland with them. These Indians created a sensation in Amsterdam which helped to spur further interest in the River Mauritius, so named for Prince Maurice.

The captors called the young men Valentine and Orson, from a medieval romance popular at the time. (The story tells of twin brothers who were separated as infants. Valentine was brought up at a prince's court; Orson was carried off by a she-bear and reared as a rough child of nature. Ultimately they were reunited.)

With the knowledge they now had, Christiaensen and Block readily found backing from three wealthy merchants for an expedition to plant a trading post on the river. Two ships—the *Fortune,* commanded by Christiaensen, and the *Tiger,* under Block—set sail in the summer of 1613. They took Valentine and Orson back with them. The two Indians were held at Fort Nassau, possibly as interpreters.

There was ample reason for these traders to choose Castle Island. An Indian village stood at the mouth of the Normanskill, just opposite the island. The Normanskill valley was part of the Mohawks' overland route from Schenectady to the Hudson. No doubt, too, the Dutchmen felt themselves safer from surprise attack on an island. (They had yet to learn of the annual floods which would plague Albany until the Sacandaga Reservoir.)

We know the fort was begun, if not completed, before the end of 1613, because the Christiaensen-Block expedition wintered there. Fort Nassau took the form of a redoubt—58 feet wide between walls, and

8 FLASHBACK

surrounded by a moat 18 feet wide. A house 38 feet long and 26 feet wide was erected inside the walls. Two cannon and eleven swivels served as protection.

Sometime during that winter, Block's ship, the *Tiger,* was burned. Block and his crew replaced it with a smaller one, the *Onrust* (Restless). With this Block explored Long Island Sound, giving his own name to the beautiful island near the Sound's eastern end.

Leaving Jacob Eelkens in command of Fort Nassau, the two captains sailed back down the river when it opened in the spring of 1614. They arrived in Holland that July. Eelkens, a former clerk in an Amsterdam counting house, carried on a thriving business and periodically sent a shallop loaded with furs down the river to Manhattan for transshipment to the homeland.

On the basis of what Christiaensen and Block reported, and the splendid furs they brought, the Amsterdam merchants sought a trade monopoly of the river. At a meeting of the States-General of the Netherlands in October, they applied for a charter granting such rights, submitting a map drawn by Captain Block, the famed "Carte Figuratif," showing Fort Nassau. The New Netherland Company was chartered with the exclusive right to make four trading voyages before 1619.

While furs poured in to Fort Nassau, scouting parties set out to explore the adjacent country. One such party went out the Mohawk Valley, located the headwaters of the Delaware River, and canoed down that river as far as the Schuylkill in Pennsylvania.

Captain Christiaensen later returned to Fort Nassau. The Indian lad called Orson had become bad tempered. He was described as "an exceedingly malignant wretch." During an argument, he killed Christiaensen. The scant records say merely that he was "repaid with a bullet as his reward."

The Hudson River misbehaved dramatically in the spring breakup of 1617, nearly sweeping Fort Nassau away. The proprietors thereupon moved their trading post over to the mainland, adjacent to the Indian village. They kept the name Fort Nassau for seven years; then a new fort farther north became Fort Orange. Appropriately enough, the site of Fort Nassau is occupied now by the Port of Albany, focus of mercantile commerce.

Adapted from "Fort Nassau," *Times Union,* September 20, 1964 (special supplement).

1690

★ ★ ★ ★ ★ ★ ★ ★ ★ ★ ★ ★

Massacre at Schenectady

THE WAR PARTY HEADING for Albany numbered 210 men. Of these, 114 were Frenchmen, mostly tough coureurs-de-bois (woods runners). Titular leader of the party was Le Moyne de Sainte Helene, assisted by one of his ten brothers, Le Moyne d'Iberia, and by D'Aillebout de Mantet. The rest were Indians.

They departed Montreal on January 17. Wearing snowshoes and hauling provisions on handsledges, they tramped down the ice of Lake Champlain. The 22-day march was made even more grueling by an unseasonable thaw. After leaving the lake, they plodded through forest and bog slush to their knees. The floundering column must have left a readily discernible trail, but Mohawk scouts unaccountably missed them. A few days on the way, the Indians, from whom the destination had been kept secret, demanded to know where they were going. At the reply, "Orange" (the French usage for Albany), an Indian asked: "How long is it since the French grew so bold?"

The warriors all knew that Albany was defended by a fort with cannon. The Indians muttered that the party was not strong enough to attack it. Where Schuylerville is today, the trail forked, one path leading to Albany, the other to Schenectady. At that point, the Indians bluntly refused to tackle Albany. Thereby they doomed Schenectady, the stockade they called Corlaer for its founder, Arendt Van Curler.

As the party came down from the Ballston Lake valley, they paused to warm themselves at the fire of four squaws and asked for directions. An advance scouting party was sent ahead and came back to report they "saw no one." In a rising gale, the troop pressed on until, from the Glenville hills, they could see the lights of the stockade beyond the Mohawk River.

It was 11 o'clock the night of Saturday, February 8, 1690. The leaders had planned the attack for 2 a.m., but their men were stiff from the cold wind, unable to build a fire lest it betray their presence, and refused to wait. Silently they moved down the slopes and crossed the river ice. To their surprise, they found the stockade gates wide open and completely unguarded. Probably the winter storm had lulled the residents into carelessness, along with the fact that a garrison of 25 Connecticut militia was quartered inside. Snow had fallen heavily the day before, lying three feet deep on the level and drifting in the narrow lanes between dwellings. Legend has it that the raiders found two snowmen—imitation sentinels—posted outside the north gate.

The high palisaded walls of the Schenectady stockade were 660 feet long on a side, and enclosed between 40 and 60 houses. Most of the 300 inhabitants were Dutch, and they had gone to bed early. The attackers entered by the north gate stealthily around midnight. Observing strict silence, they split into two files and stole along the east and west palisade walls to rejoin at the south gate. They infiltrated the streets, five or six men taking up stations before the door of every house. At the signal of an Indian whoop, the raiders entered all houses simultaneously. The occupants barely had time to get out of bed. How few of them were able to reach weapons is attested by the fact that only two of the intruders were killed and one badly wounded.

A French officer with a detachment burst into the small fort at one corner, killing four of the militia men including the commanding officer, Lieutenant Talmadge, and capturing five. Another Frenchman, M. de Montigny, invading a home with his sword drawn, received two spear thrusts from the master of the house. The leader, Le Moyne, came to his aid, and they "put everyone in that house to the sword."

Stout Adam Vrooman, after seeing his wife and child killed before his eyes (the wife shot and burned, the child's head bashed against the door post), barricaded himself with his musket and put up such a fight that the enemy made a "peace pact" with him.

At the outset, Simon Schermerhorn, age 32, slipped out a back way, mounted his horse, and spurred for the north gate. As he went through, a French rifleman spotted him and fired. Simon took a bullet in his thigh and the horse was wounded, but he kept on, bent upon carrying the alarm to Albany and getting help. Schermerhorn took the Niskayuna Path along the Mohawk to alert some forts on the river and then veered to Albany, a total distance of 20 miles. He made the Albany gate, half dead, at 5 a.m.

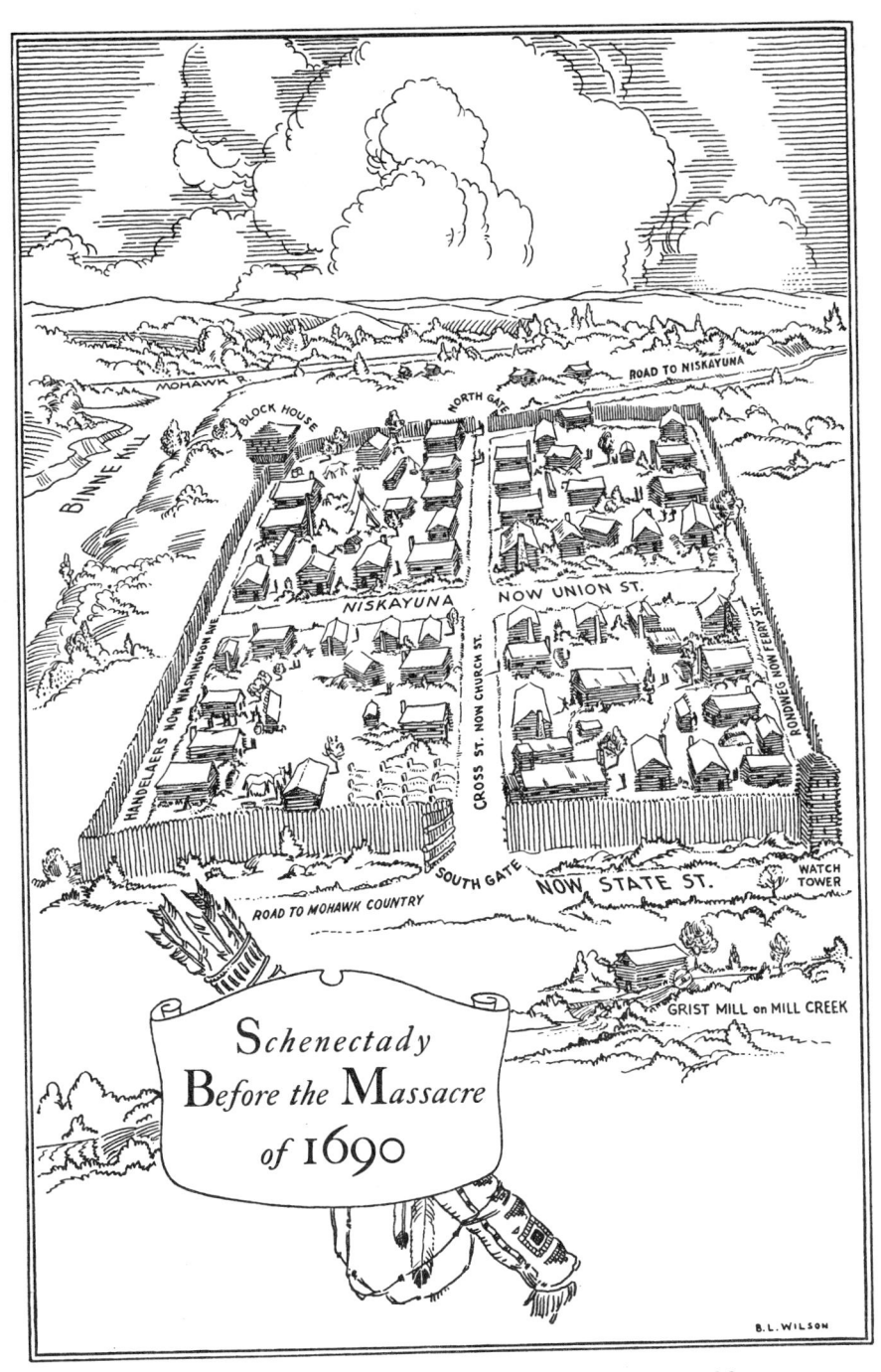

The Schenectady stockade seemed secure and safe in 1690.

This midnight ride of Simon Schermerhorn was actually more of a feat than Paul Revere's celebrated journey. It was miles longer and taken under much more adverse conditions—horse and rider wounded, wind and snow hindering progress, the rider inadequately dressed. Gasping, brave Simon—who, of course, had no chance to count the raiders—reported there were more than 1,000 French and Indians. Albany fell into a panic. All men reported to post. The fort fired several guns to warn the outlying farmers.

Twenty-five Schenectady refugees struggled into Albany during the day, some with frozen hands and feet. Mayor Pieter Schuyler ordered some scouts forth on horseback to reconnoitre, but they found the snow so deep they turned back. (Schermerhorn had made it!)

Within two hours, 60 people (38 men, 10 women, 12 children) had been slain in Schenectady. All but five or six houses had been burned. (Those were spared presumably so the tired raiders would have a place to sleep before heading home.)

Next morning a deputation of Frenchmen called on Captain John Sander Glen, at his home on the Scotia side of the river. By specific orders, his family and home had been spared because he had earlier befriended escaped French prisoners of the Mohawk Indians. He was invited to come over to identify any of his kinfolk among the cowering prisoners. He claimed so many that the Indians indignantly protested that he could not possibly have that many relatives.

The French did not loiter. They gathered 50 horses and loaded them with plunder. Taking 27 able-bodied prisoners with them, they began the retreat at 11 a.m. Sunday, February 9. On the way home they killed and ate 34 of the horses. Two days later, angry Mohawks swarmed into the Schenectady stockade to inspect the sad scene. They promised to help their surviving friends rebuild. Mohawk warriors joined 50 young men from Albany in pursuit of the raiders. They overtook some stragglers and killed 14.

The Schenectady Massacre was actually the opening gun in the series of four French-and-Indian wars. On this continent it signaled the beginning of what Americans knew as King William's War, but which across the Atlantic was a European war mainly between England and France.

The ordeal of Schenectady jolted the colonies in a way the French had not foreseen. It forced them to realize that they could not rely on a government overseas for their defense. It put them on notice that a primary aim of the French in Canada was to gain control of the Hudson

River and thus split New England off from the rest of the British colonies. It may be said that Schenectady's tragedy inspired the first faint glimmering of the idea of union in these colonies.

Adapted from "270 Years Ago: the Schenectady Massacre," *Times Union,* February 7, 1960.

1754

★ ★ ★ ★ ★ ★ ★ ★ ★ ★ ★ ★ ★ ★

The Fear of Attack

RECURRENT THUNDERSTORMS drenched the first few days of the palaver, pushing the Hudson over its banks. Delegates not used to this headstrong river eyed the flood uneasily as it ripped a dozen sloops from their moorings and inched near the top of the log pilings. The Stadt Huys where they met was on low ground near the docks.

Perhaps some of the nervous onlookers read into the swirling water the ominous rising of the French menace against the weak northern and western frontiers of the English colonies. The breath of war was hot on the neck of this meeting. Indeed, some blood had already been shed in the wilds of Pennsylvania.

The convention was five days behind schedule in opening. A New England representative arrived with an excruciating toothache that allowed him no sleep. Delegations bickered over the order of their seating. Indian attendants drifted in belatedly, sullenly. The key tribe of the Iroquois—the Mohawks, with only 40 miles to travel—were a full two weeks late. Their lame excuse suggested that the delay was deliberate, a statement of disrespect for the conveners.

Thus inauspiciously did the Albany Congress of 1754 get under way. It lasted 23 days, counting Sundays when the colonial representatives went to church. It was a worried and somewhat desperate gathering. With France threatening to take over America, the British were hastily mending their fences. The colonies badly needed the help of the Iroquois Confederacy, and the Indians were "of a wavering disposition."

Tension gripped the town, with hundreds of Indians milling in the streets and camping on the hill outside the gates. The residents were anxious for the meetings to begin and end. Their concern grew when they heard that a French Indian had "sneaked into the city under cover of the confusion and was seen prowling around the Albany house of

William Johnson [the valuable go-between with the Iroquois], taking the measure of its walls." Their concern was well founded. King Hendrick, the Mohawk sachem, reporting the episode to the Congress, said: "We think him [Johnson] in very great danger, because the French will take more than ordinary pains either to kill him or to take him prisoner on account of his great interest among us."

The primary purpose of the Albany Congress was to conciliate the Iroquois and dissuade them from going over to the French side, as some had already done. Johnson's relationship with the Iroquois was a slender thread on which all this hung.

The call to the colonies went out April 19, 1754, from Governor William Shirley of Massachusetts, who added this as a secondary aim: "also for entering into Articles of Union and Confederation . . . for the general defence of his Majesty's subjects and interests in North America."

Seven colonies sent commissioners to the Congress, a total of 25 of the more distinguished men in British America. Represented were New Hampshire, Massachusetts Bay, Rhode Island, Connecticut, Pennsylvania, Maryland, and New York. (The Virginia Assembly refused to vote expenses for a delegation. New Jersey ignored the summons. Rhode Island and Connecticut came without invitation.)

Emissaries went out in advance to the Six Nations of the Iroquois to cajole them into attending the pow-wow for the purpose of "burying the hatchet and renewing the covenant chain." The Indians had been disgruntled since they had walked out, "in an abrupt and hasty manner," on a meeting in New York the previous summer. The Lords of Trade and Plantations in London, anxious to placate them, had sent a letter in September, 1753, ordering the Congress at Albany.

Between the date of this notice and the opening session on June 19, an incident in the Pennsylvania forest intensified the urgency. The treaty ending King George's War six years before had been little more than a truce; everyone knew it was but a question of time until a real showdown between France and England erupted. Governor Dinwiddle of Virginia had sent a small militia company to the Forks of the Ohio (future site of Pittsburgh) to learn what the French were doing and to build a fort. He had placed an inexperienced planter-aristocrat of 22, George Washington by name, in command. On May 28, Washington's men fired on a French reconnaissance party, and its leader, Jumonville, was killed. France charged "assassination" of a peaceful envoy. The avenging French attacked Washington's contingent at Fort Necessity, forcing its surrender on July 4. The bad news reached Albany just before the Congress adjourned, and lent impetus to the homeward dash of the alarmed delegates.

The Albany Congress was presided over by the acting Governor of New York, James De Lancey. The former Chief Justice had been appointed Lieutenant Governor the previous fall, on the arrival of Sir Danvers Osborne from England as Governor. Two days after taking office, the new Governor had hanged himself in New York, presumably in grief over the recent death of his wife.

Right-hand man to De Lancey was William Johnson, baronial overlord of the Mohawk Valley and compassionate friend to the Iroquois. His attendance at the Albany Congress had much to do with bringing in the reluctant Indians. They were furious because the government had recently relieved Johnson of his position as Indian agent and replaced him with a Board of Indian Commissioners at Albany. A Mohawk spokesman demanded that Johnson be reinstated "for we love him and he us, and he has always been our good and trusty friend."

The Congress was called to order on June 19, with the delegates gathered around a large table in the old Stadt Huys. It was a grand occasion. According to historian George Bancroft: "America had never seen an assembly so venerable for the states represented or for the great and able men that composed it." The Indian business came first—but there were as yet few Indians in evidence. About 200 Iroquois arrived on June 22. It was not until June 28 that King Hendrick and his Mohawks showed up.

The first several days were spent drafting a careful speech to mollify the Indians who complained that they were being defrauded of their lands, that their interests were being neglected, and that Albany traders were smuggling guns and powder to the French at Montreal. Even while the Indians were being reassured inside, land-grabbers outside the Stadt Huys were plying them with rum and inducing them to sign away the Wyoming Valley in Pennsylvania—a swindle that later turned into tragedy.

Much pompous oratory took place, punctuated by the exchange of belts and strings of wampum, the tokens of fealty to the Indians; and by the "Yo-Heigh-Eigh" which the Indians intoned in unison as a kind of applause. Of course, each speaker had to pause for the interpreters—and the translations were not very good.

The strongest speech of the Congress was made by the Mohawk chief, King Hendrick, then 75 years old. (He was killed the following year in the Bloody Morning Scout at Lake George.) Hendrick was bitter and blunt. "This is the ancient place of treaty where the fire of friendship always used to burn," he said, with a sweeping gesture to take in

Albany. "And 'tis now three years since we have been called to any public treaty here. . . . 'Tis your fault, Brethren, that we are not strengthened by conquest, for we would have gone and taken Crown Point, but you hindered us. . . . Instead of this, you burnt your own fort at Saratoga and run (sic) away from it, which was a shame and a scandal to you. Look about your country and see. You have no fortification about you, no not even to this city. 'Tis but one step from Canada hither, and the French may easily come and turn you out of your doors."

Hendrick picked up a stick, broke it in pieces and tossed it over his shoulder. "You have thrown us behind your back and disregarded us," he chided the white dignitaries, who must have been squirming in their seats; "whereas the French are a subtle and a vigilant people . . . walking softly like the wolf in winter to seduce and bring our people over to them.

"You were desirous that we should open our minds and our hearts to you. Look at the French; they are men, they are fortifying everywhere. But, we are ashamed to say it, you are all like women—bare and open, without any fortification."

The Congress replied: "We are very sorry that any neglect has been shown to you, and we hope that nothing of that kind will happen hereafter. You are old and steady friends. . . . The covenant is renewed, the chain is brightened, the fire burns clear."

A wealth of gifts had been brought to Albany for the Indians by each delegation and an especially lavish one from the King. Included in this were 400 guns and much powder. The Indians went away at least half mollified and came over to the side of the colonies when war broke loose.

The next item on the agenda was the Plan of Union. The idea of a federation of the colonies was not a new one. The United Colonies of New England had set a precedent as far back as 1643. Such men as William Penn and Daniel Coxe had drawn up schemes of union. Governor Shirley had one, and several delegates, including Benjamin Franklin, came to Albany with such plans under their hats. Franklin had considered a union necessary for a long time. He had begun hinting at the union proposal in 1751 in his Philadelphia newspaper. He had printed what was probably the first newspaper cartoon—showing a rattlesnake cut up into pieces, with the slogan "Join or Die." "We must unite or be overcome," he editorialized the month prior to the meeting. Franklin had worked out details of his plan during the journey to Albany.

It was no idealistic dream of a united nation that underlay such an idea; these colonies were intensely competitive and jealous of one another. It was plain fear of attack.

Early in the proceedings, on June 24, the delegates had voted this resolution: "Resolved, that a union of all the colonies is absolutely necessary for their security and defense." During all the Indian proceedings, a committee appointed to consider a plan for union, with Franklin as its chairman, had been deliberating in the background. Just before the Congress broke up on July 11, it adopted a plan—essentially Franklin's, with some modifications.

The plan was to be taken back to the Assemblies of the several colonies for their approval before being submitted to the English Parliament. It never got that far. The Assemblies knocked it down, one by one. The colonial bigwigs thought it conceded too much to the Crown. More importantly, each colony balked at surrendering any of its own interests to a central government.

Even if the Albany Plan had reached Parliament, it probably would have been scotched there as being dangerously democratic. This would have been ironic. The Albany Plan held no thought of independence from England. It is more than likely that, had the Albany Plan succeeded, there would have been no Declaration of Independence. The idea was simply for the colonies to band together, in complete loyalty to the British crown, for military defense. If they had done so then, England perhaps would not have levied the onerous taxes that provoked the Revolution.

The best simple definition of the plan is to be found in Franklin's own words: "By this plan the general government was to be administered by a president general, appointed and supported by the crown, and a Grand Council was to be chosen by the representatives of the people of the several colonies, met in their respective assemblies." Of course there was much more to the plan, including the powers to govern Indian affairs, to raise a common army, and to levy taxes for its support.

Benjamin Franklin wrote afterward in his *Autobiography:* "The different and contrary reasons of dislike of my plan makes me suspect that it was really the true medium, and I am still of the opinion it would have been happy for both sides of the water if it had been adopted. The colonies, so united, would have been sufficiently strong to have defended themselves. There would then have been no need of troops from England; of course, the subsequent pretence for taxing America and the bloody events it occasioned, would have been avoided."

Although Franklin was never faulted for excessive humility, he may have been correct here.

Adapted from "Albany Congress was 'Cradle of Union,'" *Times Union,* April 25, 1954.

1804

★ ★ ★ ★ ★ ★ ★ ★ ★ ★ ★ ★ ★ ★

The Infamous Duel

GENERAL PHILIP SCHUYLER, aged 70, lay gravely ill in his lordly but lonely Albany mansion when the shattering word reached him that Alexander Hamilton had been killed in a duel with Aaron Burr. It came as a letter from another of his sons-in-law, John Barker Church, to whose wife, Angelica, he then wrote that the news "affected me so deeply as to threaten serious results."

As a matter of fact this family tragedy did apparently hasten his own demise. Hamilton died July 12, 1804, after being carried to the home of a friend, William Bayard, in Greenwich Village. The great Revolutionary general reached his end four months later, on November 18. Alexander Hamilton, the first U.S. Secretary of the Treasury, had been more like a real son to him than a son-by-marriage, as well as his closest confidant and political ally.

To compound the shock, the fatal bullet had been fired by a man who had been introduced to Hamilton 23 years earlier by Schuyler himself, in this same Georgian mansion, "The Pastures." Aaron Burr, as a temporary resident of Albany in 1782 while preparing to pass a bar exam, was a frequent and welcome guest in the Schuyler home, on social terms with the master's wife and daughters, and was permitted free access to Schuyler's large and excellent library.

After the British evacuated New York City in 1783, both Hamilton and Burr moved into Manhattan to practice law, in a town where long enemy occupation had left a multiplicity of legal problems in its wake. They rose rapidly in their chosen profession, sometimes appeared together in the same courtrooms, either as opponents or collaborators on cases. But their paths diverged politically.

The ailing General, incapacitated by his recurrent malady, the gout, must have been reminded of this and other past relations with Burr as he took up his pen to console his abruptly widowed daughter, Elizabeth Hamilton, in New York. With unsteady hand, he wrote:

"My dear Eliza—This morning Mr. Church's letter has announced to me the severe affliction which it has pleased the Supreme Being to inflict upon you, on me and on all dear to us. If aught under Heaven could aggravate the affliction I experience, it is that, incapable of moving or being moved, I can not fly to you to pour the balm of comfort into your afflicted bosom, to water it with my tears, and to receive yours on mine."

This was the latest of a crescendo of woes that had befallen Schuyler in the past five years. First had been the death of his daughter, Margarita, the wife of Patroon Stephen Van Rensselaer. Then his bright and promising grandson and namesake, Philip Hamilton—20-year-old son of the Hamiltons—was killed in a duel which ominously foreshadowed his father's fate. In that case, Philip had issued the challenge to an attorney named George Eacker, politically hostile to the Hamilton-Schuyler faction, for publicly attacking his father's reputation. That duel was fought in November, 1801, on the Weehawken, New Jersey, dueling grounds, the same notorious location to which Aaron Burr three years later challenged Alexander Hamilton.

The deep sorrow of the prior tragedy had hardly dissipated when, in 1803, the General's beloved wife—the former Catherine ("Sweet Kitty") Van Rensselaer—died unexpectedly. Since that bereavement, Schuyler had turned ever more to the Hamiltons for solace, writing them: "I am aware that nothing tends so much to the alleviation of distress as the endearing attention of children."

It may be that Hamilton and Burr had crossed paths as young officers in the Continental Army during Washington's retreat across Manhattan from Brooklyn Heights in 1776. Burr was with Washington at Valley Forge during the dismal winter that ensued. Hamilton later was an aide-de-camp to Washington, and was on his staff at Morristown, New Jersey, the winter of 1779–80 when the army suffered even more, especially from hunger. There Hamilton first met, courted, and won the hand of Elizabeth (Betsey) Schuyler, second of the five daughters of General Philip Schuyler.

Schuyler had recently taken his seat as a member of the Continental Congress, and brought his wife and younger daughters to Philadelphia with him. Betsey had stayed behind, to come on later, stopping in Morristown for a visit with an aunt who was wife of the surgeon-general. An attractive and vivacious young lady, Betsey caught Hamilton's eye during dances and social events. It was a whirlwind courtship, and she had already accepted his proposal by the time Schuyler arrived at the encampment as one of a congressional committee to inspect the army's needs. The General gave his consent, on condition the wedding be postponed until it could be performed at home in Albany. The couple were married at "The Pastures" mansion on December 14, 1780.

Hamilton continued on military duty after his marriage, and was a lieutenant-colonel when he led a heroic assault in the siege of Cornwallis at Yorktown. He was in command of a battalion which stormed one of the key redoubts of the British defenses. Under heavy fire, Hamilton leaped to the parapet, called his men to follow, and was first into the works. Lord Cornwallis surrendered on October 19, 1781.

Hamilton left for Albany within a week of the surrender. According to Schuyler, "he thought of nothing but reaching [his wife] the soonest possible, and indeed he tyred his horses to accomplish it, and was obliged to hire others to come on from Red Hook."

Although the peace treaty was not signed until 1783, Hamilton now withdrew from the military to accept an appointment by Robert Morris with the new federal Office of Finance, but more than incidentally to prepare himself for the practice of law. Aaron Burr, who had left the army in 1780 for health reasons, was pursuing the same goal and his path led him to Albany.

Many pre-war barristers had been Tories or British Loyalists, and the New York Legislature, in 1780, passed a law to prohibit remaining Tories from practicing law until 1786. A huge backlog of legal cases had been piling up during the Revolution, and many more would arise out of it. Hence the legal profession was a beckoning field for young men coming out of uniform. Burr and an ex-army friend, Robert Troup, set about studying for it together by reading law in Litchfield, Connecticut, when the Battle of Bunker Hill set him ablaze with patriotism.

Aaron Burr had a notable family background, in the ministry. He was the son and grandson (in that order) of the first two presidents of Princeton University. The grandfather was the celebrated New England Calvinist divine, the Rev. Jonathan Edwards, who was appointed the new college's head when his son died in the office. Later on, Aaron himself sailed through Princeton with scholastic ease.

When war broke out, Burr rode for Cambridge to enlist in the ragtail army over which George Washington had just taken command for the siege of Boston. He was with Benedict Arnold's torturous wilderness march up the Kennebec River and over into Canada for the ill-starred attack on Quebec.

Back in civilian life, both these veterans faced the same hurdle.

Admittance to the bar was granted by the State Supreme Court of Judicature, which alternated its semiannual terms between Albany and New York City. In the fall and winter, 1781-82, the court was sitting in Albany. By standard rule, a license to practice law required at least three years of clerkship (reading law) under a qualified instructor. Owing to the urgent need for attorneys as the war was winding down, the court had relaxed this rule "in favor of such young Gentlemen who had directed their Studies to the profession of the Law, but upon the breaking out of the present War had entered into the defence of their Country." Such exceptions, however, must have the unanimous consent of all three sitting judges. Hamilton and Burr were in the same boat.

Burr could claim no more than twelve months of legal studies. In the autumn of 1781 he hied himself to Albany with the idea of gaining personal audiences with the three sitting judges, one at a time, but he met with long delays in getting to them. His fellow applicant, Robert Troup, came with him; Troup was also an army friend of Hamilton's.

It was a tough winter. During this time of waiting, Burr did not suffer unduly from boredom. His background and social charm brought him invitations from the elite families of Albany, including the Van Rensselaers. (Burr was noted as a "ladies' man" all his life.) He lost no time in putting to use a letter of introduction provided him by General Alexander McDougall, under whom he had served at Valley Forge and elsewhere. The letter was addressed to General Philip Schuyler, who surveyed the sharp-looking, confident young man while he read the script:

"This will be handed you by Lt. Col. Burr, who goes to Albany to solicit a license in our courts. Being a stranger in that part of the country, I beg leave by this to introduce him to you. He is a soldier, an officer, and a worthy citizen. I am persuaded by my knowledge of him that he will merit every attention you may think proper to show him."

Schuyler reacted by welcoming Burr as a frequent guest in his home, and here Burr got on familiar terms with Hamilton and his wife. The younger men had in common their recent military life and their preparation for the law. Schuyler lent books from his private library to Burr, who later spoke of having read Rousseau that winter in Albany. (Rousseau's *Confessions* are part of that original library as preserved today in the Schuyler Mansion.)

Hamilton was aided by Robert Troup in his cramming for the bar exam. Both Burr and Troup were slightly ahead of Hamilton in getting their licenses, and opened law offices in Albany. Hamilton did likewise

Aaron Burr felled Alexander Hamilton with a single bullet.

before summer's end. All three new-fledged lawyers were marking time for the British evacuation of New York City. Burr returned briefly to New Jersey and brought back a bride, Theodosia Prevost, widow of a British officer who had died of a fever while fighting in the Carolinas. (Theodosia was ten years Aaron's senior.)

Meanwhile Hamilton became a father and was elected to the Continental Congress by the New York Legislature. On the eve of his departure for Philadelphia, leaving his wife and infant behind with the Schuylers, he wrote his friend, the Marquis de Lafayette: "I am going to throw away a few months more on public life, and then retire a simple citizen and good pater familias." His crystal ball was badly clouded.

After a protracted session, helping to mould the shape of the young republic, Hamilton returned to the bosom of his family in August, 1783. A stay in the Schuyler home "was always a recruitment of Hamilton's powers and plans." But this interval was brief and busy, as he had law work to do, and the British were timed to pull out of New York on November 25. He learned that Burr and his wife, Theodosia, were readying to move into the city shortly before the occupation ended. The Hamiltons stepped up their schedule, with the result that they were settled at 57 Wall Street (both home and office) about the same time. In the early years of their New York residence, the two couples were on friendly terms, visiting back and forth, often dining together.

Both men prospered well, being among the most brilliant of the postwar crop of new attorneys. Chancellor James Kent, after observing most of them in action, rated Burr among the best of the lot, depicting him as "acute" and "terse." "But among all his brethren," Kent asserted, "Colonel Hamilton was indisputably preeminent," known for his grasp and frankness, and particularly active in "the claims of real property."

But the public life Hamilton had foresworn would not leave him off the hook, and Burr picked up the virus of political ambition. As a biographer has said: "Once wholly committed to politics, Burr would become a chronic office seeker."

When George Washington took oath as first President in 1789, he picked Hamilton, his favorite former aide, to be Secretary of the Treasury. In that crucial office, Hamilton maintained his close bond with Schuyler, and they saw eye-to-eye on how the nation's fiscal structure should be formulated. They agreed in the view that a government ought to be operated by those best equipped for the task; in essence, the privileged, the aristocratic uppercrust. While not disavowing democracy, Hamilton had a basic distrust of "the people," en masse, in ability to rule themselves. Between the great Hudson River families and the early New England statesmen, the Federalist Party evolved, dedicated to a strong central government, with Hamilton as its chief spokesman.

Under Federalist control, the Legislature elected New York's first two U. S. Senators in 1789, and one was inevitably Philip Schuyler. But anti-Federalist currents were at work in a coalition between Governor George Clinton and the powerful Livingston clan. When Schuyler's short term was up in 1791, this group schemed to unseat him, as an indirect slap at Hamilton. Burr was serving ably as Clinton's attorney-general. He was widely liked and politically unaligned. They drew him into the plot, and he was not averse to taking a big jump into the U. S. Senate. By devious manipulations in the Legislature, this happened. Schuyler was, so to speak, booted out by Aaron Burr. Thus began a rift that widened with the years.

Hamilton was infuriated, and he wrote in a letter: "Mr. Burr's integrity as an individual is not unimpeached. As a public man, he is one of the worst sort—a friend to nothing but as it suits his interest and ambition. Determined to climb to the highest honors of the State, and as much higher as circumstances may permit, he cares nothing about the means of effecting his purpose. 'Tis evident that he aims at putting himself at the head of what he calls the 'popular party' as affording the best tools for an ambitious man to work with, secretly turning liberty into ridicule."

From then until Burr silenced him with a bullet, Hamilton never missed a chance to speak against him, impugning his ethics, his honesty, even his private morals.

Out of that anti-Federalist movement and opposition to Hamilton's fiscal policies sprouted a second political party, the Democratic-Republican (or, as it was first called, the Republican). Virginia's Thomas Jefferson emerged as its leader. But Burr did not fit the pattern. A loner by nature, he entered the Senate as a political freelance. Performing independently, he became widely suspect in both political camps. He made forays back to his home state seeking a foothold to supplant George Clinton as Governor, to no avail as Clinton won a sixth term.

Meanwhile, Washington had accepted a second term as President. Hamilton resigned as Secretary of the Treasury in 1795, retiring to his law practice. The Federalists got back into the saddle at Albany in 1797, with John Jay as Governor and control of the Legislature. The

Legislature sent Philip Schuyler back to the U. S. Senate, when Burr's term ended, but this triumph was short-lived. Declining health soon compelled Schuyler to resign his seat.

Having tasted politics, Burr could not content himself again with a mere private life. In April, 1797, he took a comedown with election to the New York Assembly. In the interim, Thomas Jefferson had become Vice-President, under John Adams, and was casting about for supporters in a possible try for the presidency in 1800. He initiated a correspondence with Aaron Burr, up there in Albany, which had historic consequences. Jefferson sensed in Burr a potential ally toward swinging Republican votes in New York State. Burr wrote back that, generally speaking, his views coincided with those of the Vice-President. Within the month, Burr was in Philadelphia, closeted with Jefferson and some associates.

The drama built inexorably toward its climax when the Republican (i.e., Democratic) party nominated Thomas Jefferson for the presidency in 1800—and Aaron Burr for Vice-President. After the popular election, the Electoral College machinery went somehow awry. The electors met to finalize the process, but their vote came out a tie: 73 for Jefferson, 73 for Burr. As things were handled then, the man with the most electoral votes would be President. The tie vote threw the choice into the House of Representatives. The nation faced a crisis. There was no question the party leadership had intended the presidency to go to Jefferson, but the House was dominated by Federalists. Amid high suspense, the House went into closed session in February, 1801. Through an exasperating series of 29 ballotings, the tie remained unbroken. On the 30th ballot, through a stratagem, the vote finally tilted to Jefferson.

Aaron Burr was Vice-President of the United States. And Alexander Hamilton, though out of office, was still the recognized kingpin of the Federalists.

Jefferson and Burr did not work well together in tandem. Indeed, the new President developed some actual dislike for his team-mate. To the surprise of the right-wing politicians, Jefferson's outstanding achievements in office made his nomination for a second term in 1804 a certainty, but Burr knew he was going to be shelved. George Clinton, finishing his seventh term as New York Governor, was his replacement. Burr looked around for a soft place to land. What better spot than the job Clinton was vacating? He could not expect a party nomination, so Burr chose to run for the governorship as an independent. His defeat at the polls was humiliating. The state election had been in April, 1804, and he would continue as Vice-President until March, 1805. It was clear that Jefferson would not give him a cabinet post. He was facing a political dead end.

Burr came to the boiling-point, and felt like lashing out at his opponents. His rage drew a focus on a single individual who, for him, embodied them all. The "code duello" was still in covert practice, if under mounting public revulsion. President Jefferson abhorred it as "the most barbarous of appeals." New York State had made dueling a capital crime, while the issuing or accepting of a challenge was a misdemeanor. Gentlemen of New York City who felt obliged to avenge their "honor" in that fashion adopted the ruse of rowing across the Hudson to New Jersey, where a duel was not yet criminal. The obscure dueling place was a narrow ledge on the heights of Weehawken, not far from today's west entrance to the Holland Tunnel.

Burr's nemesis, Alexander Hamilton, had lately given him a fresh pretext. At a private dinner party in the Albany home of Judge John Tayler (who was later to be Lieutenant Governor under DeWitt Clinton), Hamilton had spoken out strongly against Burr for Governor. He had not expected a leak. Among the guests was Dr. Charles D. Cooper, Judge Tayler's son-in-law, who could not resist repeating bits of the conversation in two letters. The first went to Andrew Brown, an Albany merchant residing in Berne, saying: "Our Hamilton has come out decidedly against Burr. Indeed, when he was here, he spoke of him as a dangerous man, who ought not to be trusted with the reins of government."

The second letter was to Hamilton's father-in-law, Philip Schuyler. In it, Cooper wrote that he could report "a still more despicable opinion which Hamilton had expressed of Burr." The latter phrase actually triggered the duel. By some means never explained, both letters found their way into print in the Albany *Register,* and hence reached the eye of Aaron Burr.

On June 18, Burr wrote Hamilton a crisp note requesting "a prompt, unqualified acknowledgment or denial of the use of any expressions which would warrant the assertions of Dr. Cooper." Hamilton replied with a fairly long letter which seemed to skirt the issue. Burr wrote a still more specific demand, referring to the term "despicable." Again Hamilton hedged. Burr's next move, inevitably, was a challenge.

As the man challenged, Hamilton had choice of weapons. He chose pistols, and borrowed a set from his brother-in-law, John Barker Church, who had used them in England before coming to America. Hamilton drew up his will and wrote a letter for his wife. Seconds were named, who arranged the date for the duel—July 11, 1804. Hamilton told his second he intended to withhold fire. The parties met at 7 a.m. and went through the prescribed ritual. Burr drew deadly aim and hit his enemy in the abdomen.

Hamilton's pistol did go off, but the bullet clipped the twigs of a branch overhead.

In a statement left to be opened in case of his death, Hamilton said, "I was certainly desirous of avoiding this interview," and gave these reasons:

"(1) My religious and moral principles are strongly opposed to the practice of duelling, and it would ever give me pain to be obliged to shed the blood of a fellow-creature in a private combat forbidden by the laws.

"(2) My wife and children are extremely dear to me, and my life is of the utmost importance to them in various views.

"(3) I feel a sense of obligation towards my creditors. . . .

"(4) I am conscious of no ill will to Col. Burr distinct from political opposition, which, as I trust, has proceeded from pure and upright motives."

His emotional farewell lines to his wife included the words: "The scruples of a Christian have determined me to expose my own life to any extent, rather than subject myself to the guilt of taking the life of another. . . . But you had rather I should die innocent than live guilty. . . . Adieu, my darling, darling wife."

Schuyler urged Elizabeth to return to Albany, with her children, and live with him. But she chose to remain in the New York home and live out her remaining years in loneliness, preserving the memories.

A tidal wave of grief and mourning set in, with processions and mass meetings in honor of the fallen Hamilton. To an almost equal extent, Burr became an object of contempt and hatred in the public mind, the cold-blooded murderer of a national hero. Burr was stunned by the immensity of the outrage. For nearly a fortnight, he secluded himself at home, thinking it would die down, but then he took refuge under a friend's roof in Philadelphia. There he was notified that a grand jury in New York had indicted him for misdemeanor in issuing the challenge, which could mean a prison term. Then he heard that a grand jury had been called in New Jersey to indict him for murder. He might be extradited from Pennsylvania, so he decided to move on. The Vice-President of the United States was a fugitive from justice, traveling incognito. He accepted the invitation of another friend to stay for a period on St. Simons Island, off the coast of Georgia.

Hearing that the furor in the north had subsided to some degree, Burr began a leisurely return trip. When the U. S. Senate next convened on November 5, Burr appeared on the rostrum and took up the gavel to preside as if nothing had happened. He carried on as Vice-President until March 2, 1805, just before George Clinton was to succeed him. Then he made a brief valedictory speech, walked out of the chamber and closed the door on his past.

What Burr did next might supply the script for a comic operetta, except for its serious overtones. It became known as the Burr Conspiracy, and involved a complex expedition down the Ohio and Mississippi Rivers to New Orleans. Jefferson had made the Louisiana Purchase and America stood on the threshold of a great westward expansion. Burr resolved to carve a new career as part of that development. The outlines of the project he headed remain vague. Did he contemplate a personal empire and secession from the Union? Or the detachment of Texas from Mexico? Whatever the ultimate aim, the grand scheme led to his arrest and trial for treason—of which he was acquitted for lack of evidence.

But that is another story. . . . Aaron Burr had an extra public image to live down. This time he exiled himself in Europe for several years, living mainly on borrowed funds. He never got out of debt, while pursuing a variety of get-rich schemes. Finally he made his way back, obscurely, to New York and rounded out his life in the practice of law. He died in 1836 at the age of 80, and was buried in the President's Plot at Princeton.

Adapted from "Schuyler, Burr, and Hamilton Closely Linked," *Times Union,* November 21, 1954.

1860

★ ★ ★ ★ ★ ★ ★ ★ ★ ★ ★ ★ ★

Hopes Dashed

THE TELEGRAPH SPED to the *Albany Evening Journal* a dispatch from the Chicago Wigwam, the rough-boarded hall that had been nailed together to hold the Republican National Convention. The news was just in time to get under the deadline with a terse bulletin for the afternoon press run of May 19, 1860.

Frederick Seward, an associate editor, scanned the telegram with a heavy heart. It announced the defeat of high hopes for his father. Then he stepped to the speaking-tube near his desk and signalled the foreman of the composing-room. He read the words into the tube. "Abraham Lincoln is nominated for President on the third ballot." A moment's silence, and then came back the puzzled voice of the printer: "S-a-y! What damn name was that you said was nominated for President?"

The editorial staff of no newspaper in the United States felt a keener disappointment in Lincoln's nomination than that of the *Albany Evening Journal*. This paper had been the spearhead for the political aspirations of Senator William H. Seward, and Seward had been all along the odds-on favorite to win the nomination. So confident was the shrewd, cigar-smoking Senator himself that he did not even go to the convention, but sat placidly in his Auburn home composing his acceptance speech.

The Seward cohorts at the Chicago Wigwam were generaled by Thurlow Weed, the tall and imperious publisher of the *Albany Journal*. Weed was recognized as mastermind of the new Republican Party, as he had been of the old Whig Party until it was wrecked on the reefs of compromise over slavery. He was popularly regarded as a kingmaker, and his paper was closely followed in New York and Washington.

Thurlow Weed and William Seward were long-time cronies and political teammates. As the Whig "Dictator," Weed had Seward elected Governor of New York and later to the United States Senate. Now his mind was absolutely set upon making Seward the first Republican President. Thurlow Weed was not accustomed to failure.

A Seward victory was much in the air at Chicago, and premature champagne toasts were drunk to it. Even Horace Greeley, who disliked Seward and was working hard for Lincoln, wired his New York paper that Seward apparently had it sewed up. Indeed, Seward was well ahead on the first two ballots. But Lincoln's astute managers behind the scenes at the Wigwam got the bandwagon going when the Pennsylvania delegation swung to their man. Onlookers spotted tears in the eyes of the stalwart Mr. Weed when he realized he was powerless to stem the tide. He admitted in after years that he had been "annoyed and dejected" at the defeat of Seward, and could hardly wait to "shake the dust" of Chicago from his feet.

His publishing partner, George Dawson, was at Chicago with him, and presumably authored a special dispatch printed two days later by the *Albany Journal*. Signed "G. D.," the piece was filled with bitterness. "Misrepresentation has achieved its work. The timid and credulous have succumbed to threats and perversions. To please a few thousand men of equivocal principle and faltering faith, millions of loyal hearts have been saddened.

"The recognized standard bearer of the Republican Party has been sacrificed upon the altar of fancied availability. The sacrifice was alike cruel and unnecessary. No man in the Republican party has greater strength than William H. Seward. No man deserves more at the hands of that party, or possesses greater fitness for the high office for which its national tribunal has declared him worthy. . . . He was deemed too pure, too wise, and too thoroughly and too conspicuously embued with the distinctive principles of Republicanism to succeed."

G. D. grudgingly admitted that "Mr. Lincoln is a bold, gallant, and uncompromising Republican," but said that Seward's friends "deemed him greatly the inferior, in every way, of their candidate. And they said so, kindly, but with emphasis."

Two of Lincoln's managers came to Weed's hotel room, urging him to visit the nominee at Springfield (like Seward, Lincoln had remained at home) before returning to Albany. Weed replied that he was "so greatly disappointed at the result of the action of the convention as to be unable to think or talk on the subject." After simmering down on a trip to Iowa, however, Weed thought better of his decision and did stop over at Springfield, where Lincoln entertained him in his home. Of this visit, Weed wrote: "I had supposed, until we now met, that I had never seen Mr. Lincoln, having forgotten that in the fall of 1848,

William H. Seward had strong Albany support in his quest for the Presidency.

when he took the stump in New England, he called on me at Albany." Weed came away persuaded that the candidate was "sagacious and practical," at least.

Obviously Lincoln had made no great impression earlier on the great politician. At that time he had been a rather ungainly young Congressman, anxious to ingratiate himself with the Whig leaders. He had taken a swing up through New England to mend fences for the presidential candidate of that year, General Zachary Taylor. Heading back for Illinois, he had paused in Albany and sought out Mr. Weed. Together they walked up the street to call upon Millard Fillmore, State Comptroller, who was running for Vice-President with Taylor. (Fillmore soon became President when Taylor died in the White House.)

In any case, Weed and Seward now swallowed their chagrin and rallied to the support of Lincoln and his running mate, Hannibal Hamlin. The *Albany Journal* began using a woodcut daily at the top of a column showing Lincoln with axe in hand, splitting rails. It exchanged caustic insults with the *Atlas and Argus,* which trumpeted for the main Democratic nominee, Senator Stephen A. Douglas, heading its editorial column each day with the words, "Let the People be Heard."

Senator Seward actually took the stump for Lincoln and gave newsworthy speeches through the northern states. His son, Frederick, made a similar adjustment in his job at the *Journal,* actively supporting the party choice.

The Albany Wide-Awakes sprang into delighted action. The Wide-Awakes, a universal phenomenon of that Lincoln campaign, were companies of young men who marched, chanted, played bands, and drummed up votes. They wore a peculiar uniform of oilcloth capes and caps and carried blazing torches over their shoulders. The fad originated in Hartford the previous winter when Lincoln came East for his Cooper Union address. During his stop in Hartford, two drygoods clerks, about to march in a torchlight parade, got the idea of borrowing oilcloth strips out of their store, with holes for their heads, to shield their clothing from the drip of the torches.

Among Lincoln's army of workers was a singularly effective volunteer stump-speaker from Mechanicville—a magnetic youth named Elmer Ellsworth, whom Lincoln came to treat almost as an adopted son. Ellsworth had vaulted into popular acclaim earlier that same year when he toured the East in command of a remarkable drill team, the United States Zouave Cadets. He had trained this outfit to a snappy peak of perfection in Chicago. By the time the tour was finished, young ladies

Thurlow Weed used his immense power and influence to try to keep Lincoln out of the White House.

pinned his picture on their walls and wrote him fan letters. Lincoln had met Ellsworth when his Cadets gave a performance in Springfield, and had been so impressed by his radiant personality as to invite him, if ever he wished to study law, to come and enter his office.

After Lincoln's nomination, Ellsworth took Lincoln up on the offer, leaving his drill team to fall apart. But he spent more time making campaign speeches for Lincoln in Illinois than he did reading law. He also became a favorite guest in the Lincoln household, romping with the boys and winning the hearts of the parents. After the election, Lincoln asked him to accompany them to Washington, where he would get an appointment for him.

In short, Lincoln won the election, thanks to a North-South split in the Democratic Party and the flocking of enthusiastic Northerners to the Republican standard. The election was wildly celebrated in Albany. All the Wide-Awake companies of the region massed for a continuing torchlight parade that went on until midnight. Streets were decorated and public buildings and stores illumined. Cannon boomed and fireworks flared. At one downtown corner, a group of rail-splitters busily built a fence. The procession paused in front of Governor Edwin Morgan's house, 144 State Street, to salute him, and he came out on the porch and spoke. Senator Seward, who was in town, emerged to watch the marchers. They cheered him and he waved from Morgan's balcony.

Before long, at Lincoln's request, Thurlow Weed made another trip to Springfield. The President-elect explained that he wasn't much of a "cabinet-maker" and would appreciate some expert advice. Lincoln soon announced his appointment of Senator Seward as Secretary of State. Seward subsequently took his son, Frederick, out of his Albany newspaper job to become Assistant Secretary of State.

These two men appear again in this book, in the chapter, "Booth's Bullet—1865."

Adapted from "Local GOP Chiefs, Paper Changed Tune on Rail Splitter," *Times Union,* April 11, 1965.

1861

★ ★ ★ ★ ★ ★ ★ ★ ★ ★ ★ ★ ★ ★

The Gun-Toting Mayor

THE MAYOR OF ALBANY on the eve of the Civil War was a Democrat who felt—along with many of his party in the North—that the election of Abraham Lincoln was a political calamity. He favored further compromise with the South and feared the results of extremist actions. A self-made man of wealth and a broad-shouldered figure at the age of 42, this was a Mayor who, when he lifted his right hand and swore to uphold the Constitution, meant that he would uphold the Constitution. He also agreed with Voltaire's maxim: "I disapprove of what you say, but I will defend to the death your right to say it."

In brief, George Hornell Thacher was the brand of mayor who—although he had scant sympathy with the sentiments of the speakers—strode grimly up the aisle of the Anti-Slavery Convention and sat on the platform for hours with a loaded revolver in his lap to insure that the right of free speech would prevail in Albany, if in no other city of the state. This action won him a flurry of national renown. "In Albany the mayor was a man," Susan B. Anthony declared.

Although Lincoln had not yet reached Washington, Southern states were seceding. A group of Southern students at Union College abandoned their studies that week and headed for home, after running up the Palmetto Flag (state flag of South Carolina) in Schenectady. The North had a case of jitters. Many feared that rantings of radical abolitionists might precipitate the war everyone dreaded.

The Anti-Slavery Convention in Albany was to open on Monday, February 4, 1861. The previous Friday, the Democratic Constitutional Unionist Convention (attended by more than 700 delegates from all over the state) had finished its sessions here. Dismayed by the recent Republican victory at the polls, the Democrats still claimed to represent "the views and feelings of a majority of the people of New York."

They had met "to avert the threatened destruction of our National Union," and to "force a reluctant and obstructive Legislature to stand aside and let the people speak in this crisis."

Albany's venerable judge, Amasa J. Parker, the party's permanent chairman, said the Democrats had the right to insist on "conciliation, concession, compromise." Mayor Thacher had been a delegate to that convention, held in Tweddle Hall. Others were Erastus Corning, the railroad mogul; ex-Governor Horatio Seymour; and ex-Mayor Eli Perry. One speaker, who looked into the future with a badly smoked glass, had fulminated: "Civil War will not restore the Union, but will defeat forever its reconstruction."

The upshot of this fretful session was a resolution addressed to the Legislature asking it to submit the Crittenden Compromise to a vote of the people. (The Crittenden "proposition," authored by Kentucky Senator John Jordan Crittenden, would have revived the Missouri Compromise, extending the dividing line between slave and free territory all the way to the Pacific.)

On Saturday, the day after the Democrats left town, the front page of the *Atlas and Argus* carried a long message from Mayor George H. Thacher—a reply to a petition he had received. The petition said: "We earnestly entreat your interposition . . . to prevent the gathering of an association of individuals whose well-known sentiments, expressed at this time, when the country is in such a distracted condition, we fear would lead to disorderly demonstrations . . . and cast discredit upon our city."

The "association of individuals" mentioned was a group of crusaders and reformers headed by Susan B. Anthony, the famous women's rights pioneer. The fight for the emancipation of women was involved in its early phases with the abolitionist and temperance causes. In western New York, Miss Anthony had formed her league with Elizabeth Cady Stanton, Amelia Bloomer, Lucy Stone and others. As the storm-clouds of civil war grew darker, the American Anti-Slavery Society was organized to propagandize for emancipation. Susan B. Anthony, elected head of its New York State chapter in 1856, drew together a flying-squadron of speakers to hold public meetings throughout the state.

Lincoln's election, which angered the Democrats and alienated the South, also distressed the abolitionists. Lincoln, who wanted above all to preserve the Union, sounded rather mealy-mouthed to their ears; he appeared willing to leave the institution of slavery alone where it already existed.

Incensed, the Anti-Slavery Society ordered its units into action all

Mayor George H. Thacher, by securing free speech for reformers, won Susan B. Anthony's lasting respect.

along the northern front. The "100 Conventions" stormed New England; riots resulted in some places. Susan B. Anthony marshaled her forces in New York State, starting January 3 in Buffalo. The speakers were hissed, hooted, and jeered until the meeting was broken up. The pattern was repeated all the way across the state—at Rochester, Syracuse, Utica, and in smaller towns. In each instance, it appeared that local Democrats had fomented the demonstration; it was whispered that the disturbances were triggered by paid hoodlums. But most of the cities had Republican mayors who did not lift a hand to protect the speakers. Rotten eggs were hurled; red pepper was sprinkled on hot stoves in meeting halls. In Utica, Miss Anthony and her group found the hired hall locked when they arrived and nobody around to unlock it.

In not one city of the state had the Anti-Slavery Convention been permitted to have its full say. The group was to open its final meeting in Albany on February 4. Thus stood the situation when Mayor George Hornell Thacher received the petition to stop them. Thacher, founder of the Albany Car-Wheel Company, had taken office as mayor only a year earlier. (A son and a grandson would also become mayors.)

Mayor Thacher addressed his published reply "To D.V. King and 100 Other Petitioners," saying: "You do not inform me who the parties are by whom the disorderly demonstrations are likely to be made." (Here he cited his oath to uphold the Constitutions of both the nation and the state.) "Would I not violate my official oath? When and by whom was I constituted a censor over other men's opinions? . . . My own opinions and sympathies are diametrically opposed to the 'well-known sentiments' of the persons who usually compose these conventions. . . . But while I say this, I must also say that I shall most strenuously resist any and all attempts to put them down by illegal violence. Of all despotisms, the despotism of a mob is the most to be deprecated. . . . Violence is a sorry weapon with which to combat erroneous opinions. . . . No one is compelled to attend their meetings. Why then molest them?

"Let at least the Capital of the Empire State be kept free from the disgraceful proceedings which, in other localities, have brought dishonor upon our institutions. At all events, come what may, mob-law shall never prevail in our old city with my consent or connivance."

Susan B. Anthony and her colleagues arrived over the weekend and put up in the Delavan House (where Lincoln and his family would stay a fortnight later). With her were two other women whose names loom large in the annals of feminism—Elizabeth Cady Stanton and Lucretia Mott. There were also Gerrit Smith, who had provided land for John Brown's abortive fugitive slave colony in the Adirondacks; Frederick Douglass, an escaped slave making a career as an abolitionist orator; the Rev. Beriah Green; and a few other blacks.

Evidently some citizens didn't believe that Mayor Thacher meant what he said. The convention opened Monday evening in the Young Men's Association Hall, 38 State Street. Several policemen were on hand, as the crowd grew to 500. Mrs. Lucretia Mott, "a venerable Quaker lady," spoke, followed by the Rev. Beriah Green. A few hisses were heard, which soon became general, along with loud stamping of feet. The din compelled Green to retire. Gerrit Smith was called upon. The stamping was renewed. A news report said that Smith then declared his purpose to address no audience on sufferance when free speech was a right derived from the Almighty. He was urged to go on, but refused indignantly because the right had been denied to another.

Mrs. Stanton rose. She was given "a tolerable hearing" until she began criticizing "rowdies" who had disturbed the meeting in Buffalo. Then interruptions were renewed. Miss Anthony tried to speak, but "deafening" hisses and foot-stamping drowned her out. At this point, enter Mayor Thacher. "He begged the audience to remember the sacred character of free speech—and the future evils if it were trampled upon," and declared "his honest purpose to protect the rights even of those with whom he dissented." But he added, "It is also the right of any audience to applaud what they approve and to hiss that from which they dissent."

After the singing of "Hail Columbia" and "Dixie's Land," the group of speakers made their exit through a rank of policemen, over whose shoulders some jeers were heard. Next day Mayor Thacher went in person to the Delavan House to escort the crusaders to the hall. He mounted the platform with them for the afternoon sessions, warned the audience to make no disturbance, and told them that police in plain clothes were stationed throughout the hall to arrest those who disobeyed. He then sat down, pulled a revolver from his pocket, and laid it across his knees in plain sight.

An occasional subdued hiss was heard, especially when Frederick Douglass, the former slave, was speaking. The police pounced, and the hissers were ejected "with great energy and dispatch." The Mayor, with a police escort, personally accompanied the group to the hotel for dinner, back to the hall, and sat through the evening session. Later, however, he took Miss Anthony aside and said: "If you insist on holding your meeting tomorrow I shall still protect you, but it will be a difficult thing to hold this rabble in check much longer. If you will adjourn at the close of this session, I shall consider it a personal favor."

Miss Anthony acceded. But her group remained in Albany for the balance of the week to hold a Women's Rights meeting, for which the famed abolitionist, William Lloyd Garrison, arrived from New England.

An irate citizen, D. V. N. Ratcliff, wrote to the *Atlas and Argus,* saying he had left the meeting in disgust "at the offensive and insulting remarks of the Negro" (presumably Douglass), and that he had been reliably informed that Mayor Thacher had requested the Governor to detach two companies of state militia "to be used if necessary in shooting down citizens for daring to express their disapprobation, without violence, of the howling of the abolition fanatics."

The intensely biased *Atlas and Argus*—which had given extensive coverage to the Democratic Convention a few days before—completely overlooked the Anti-Slavery Convention until it was all over. Then it brayed: "The band of Abolition minstrels who have been carted through the state, performing for ten-pence admission, tried for two days to get a riot in this city, but only succeeded in getting up a row. We tried to ignore their existence, and we believe that if no notice had been taken of them, by the press or police, they would have caterwauled to empty houses. . . . These mountebanks should be treated like other showmen. They should be licensed for money, advertised where they pay for it, protected by the police, and restrained when they violate public decency. We are sorry that anyone paid any attention to them; and hope that where they next go they will be treated with contemptuous silence."

The *Atlas and Argus* did not even praise the actions of its own Democratic mayor. This remained for the leading Republican paper, the *Evening Journal,* which reported: "The right of free speech was triumphantly vindicated and mob rule effectively and promptly put down. For this great victory, our citizens are indebted to Mayor Thacher and his effective Police Force."

Adapted from "Abolitionists Gather in Albany," *Times Union,* February 5, 1961.

1861

★ ★ ★ ★ ★ ★ ★ ★ ★ ★ ★ ★ ★ ★

Lincoln and Booth

IN THE LOBBY OF STANWIX HALL, the swank hotel on Broadway, heads turned and tongues wagged when the youthful stranger with the long cloak and the drooping black moustache checked in that second weekend of February, 1861. He was so strikingly handsome as to be almost pretty, and he swept into the lobby like a performer taking the stage. His eyes and hair were black, his features delicately chiseled, his walk marked by a hint of arrogance. People saw in him a faint resemblance to the enigmatic Edgar Allan Poe. The name he signed at the register was J. Wilkes Booth.

Somewhere high above the hotel's domed roof, those three sisters, the Fates, began spinning a skein of tragedy which mortals below would not recognize until it was complete. The sinister threads were to cross shortly in Albany.

It cannot be doubted that John Wilkes Booth, age 23 and rising meteorically as an actor in the tradition of his father, Junius Brutus Booth, was anticipating his first glimpse of Abraham Lincoln in this city. Booth had been performing in theaters throughout the South, but the rising war fever had spoiled the theater business there. Booth had headed north for more lucrative engagements. (His manager assured him he could command $700 a week.) So here he was, booked in Albany as his father and elder brother had so often been, basking in the glamor and esteem which their reputations had established for him.

The newspapers told him that Lincoln would soon arrive, and surely he welcomed the chance to glimpse this man who would become the object of his hatred. Murder was not yet in the actor's heart, but malice assuredly was. For some reason the rest of his Maryland family did not fathom, he had sided hot-headedly with the South in the dispute then nearing the shooting stage. The Confederate States of America had been proclaimed only the day before in Montgomery, Alabama, with Jefferson Davis as President. The South had seized some federal forts and was threatening Fort Sumter.

Whiling away time in the hotel, Booth was not backward about letting it be known where his sympathies lay. Indeed, he talked so much on the subject that word was carried to R. K. Spackman, manager of the Gayety Theater. Worried over the possible effect on his boxoffice, he sent his treasurer, Mr. Cuyler, to chat with the high-strung actor. Finding Booth at breakfast in the hotel, Cuyler told him that unless he bridled his tongue, he would not only ruin the boxoffice but perhaps endanger his own person. With arched brows, the actor protested: "Is not this a Democratic city?"

"Democratic, yes," Cuyler replied. "But disunion, no."

Booth promised to govern his tongue while here. But he must have closely watched the daily papers as they simultaneously reported his own performances and the progress of President-elect Lincoln en route from Springfield to Washington.

In fact, the pre-inaugural trip was becoming an unprecedented spectacle. Lincoln would have preferred to travel directly to Washington from Springfield, but his political managers had arranged a zigzag course that would traverse key Northern states, with major receptions in five state capitals. There were good and sufficient reasons for the plan, to be sure. With six Southern states already seceded and threatening civil war, Northern spirits needed bolstering. Besides, it was smart public relations to allow the citizenry a personal inspection of the rough-hewn Midwesterner they had elected sight-unseen. There was enormous curiosity to see and hear the man. Lincoln accepted the invitations of five governors—those of Indiana, Ohio, Pennsylvania, New York, and New Jersey—to visit their capitals. (He declined a bid from Massachusetts, believing Boston too far a diversion.)

Not surprisingly, there was plenty of criticism of Lincoln's elaborate city-to-city swing. A Southern Congressman complained that "the forms of an imperial court" attended Lincoln's progress. The hostile Albany *Atlas and Argus* said: "We do not see why the tour was made at all. It was not necessary, and has not been usual. No other President-elect ever sought such ovations or seized such occasions for public speechmaking. . . . We fear Mr. Lincoln's triumphal procession to the capital will prove a funeral procession to his reputation." The paper described the venture as a "dizzy and devious course to Washington." There is no gainsaying that the route was roundabout. The principal cities to be visited were: Indianapolis, Cincinnati, Columbus, Pittsburgh, Cleveland, Buffalo, Albany, New York, Trenton, Philadelphia, and Harrisburg.

Lincoln and his party boarded a special train the morning Cuyler spoke to Booth. With the President-elect and Mrs. Lincoln were their three sons—Robert T., who had taken leave from his studies at Harvard to join the family; Willie and Tod; also a governess and a manservant. Lincoln bade farewell to his townsfolk at Springfield with typical brevity and humility: "Here I have lived from my youth till now I am an old man. Here the most sacred trusts of earth were assumed; here all my children were born; and here one of them lies buried. To you, dear friends, I owe all that I have, all that I am."

A resolution had gone from the New York Assembly to the Senate on January 28, 1861, saying: "Whereas, it is known that the President-elect will leave Springfield in a few days for Washington; and whereas his journey to the national capital should be marked by such manifestations of popular respect as are due as well to him as to the high office he is about to assume; and whereas the loyal people of the State of New York will cordially welcome him at every point and assure him of their devotion to the Constitution and laws of the country; therefore,

"Resolved (if the Senate concur), That His Excellency the Governor be requested to respectfully invite Mr. Lincoln to pass through this State on his way to the Federal Capital and to tender him the hospitalities of the authorities and the people."

The Senate concurred. Governor Edwin D. Morgan sent the invitation to Lincoln, who replied with customary formality on February 4: "Sir: Your letter of the 30th ultimo, inviting me, on behalf of the Legislature of New York, to pass through that state on my route to Washington, and tendering me the hospitalities of her authorities and people, has been duly received. With feelings of deep gratitude to you and them, for this testimonial of regard and esteem, I beg you to notify them that I accept the invitation so kindly extended. Your obedient servant, A. Lincoln. P.S. Please let ceremonies be only such as to take the least time possible."

The train they boarded consisted of two passenger coaches and a baggage car. The Lincoln family rode in the rear coach, a richly furnished parlor car. It would clack along over 11 different railroads to reach Washington, with a change of locomotives at each transfer point. Pilot engines ran 10 minutes ahead all the way to test the tracks. The trip, with its numerous stops and speeches, was to consume twelve days.

Second only to Lincoln himself as a celebrity aboard this train was a 23-year-old man from Mechanicville, Col. Elmer E. Ellsworth. Lincoln made his youthful protegé security officer for the journey. The instruction sheet sent ahead to local committees specified: "The President-elect will under no circumstances attempt to pass through any crowd until such arrangements are made as will meet the approval of Colonel Ellsworth, who is charged with the responsibility of all matters of this character." In other words, Lincoln was entrusting his life to Ellsworth, even though there were mature and experienced army officers on the train. Ellsworth had a formidable task. There were fears that assassination attempts would be made to prevent Lincoln from reaching Washington. Military escorts, in addition to local police, met him at every stop where he was to leave the train. Elmer, who was rather under normal stature, had a neat, dark moustache, possibly to offset his almost girlish good looks.

Incidentally, Mr. Lincoln, who had been clean-shaven all his life, had sprouted a beard with which to assume the Presidency. This, too, the opposition press derided.

Lincoln spent Tuesday, February 12, on the train crossing Indiana to Cincinnati, making speeches at numerous small-town stops. A small "filler" piece in an Albany paper noted that it was his birthday. That night, Booth performed in "The Apostate," his second play in Albany. This old-style tragedy had been especially written for Booth's father by the Irish playwright, Richard Lalor Sheil. Wilkes played his father's role, the arch-villain, Pescara. According to the stage directions, at the end of the play Pescara is stabbed and, "after a vain attempt to speak, falls dead." Booth was known for two things, his remarkable memory for his lines and his ability to make his death scenes look authentic. When the directions called for him to fall dead, the actor, Booth, athletic and in prime condition, did so most convincingly.

That night Booth accidentally wounded himself, falling in such a way that the dagger penetrated his right arm-pit. Though it was only a flesh wound, it bled a lot and kept him in the wings for a week.

On the 18th, the day Lincoln was scheduled to arrive in Albany, the paper noted that Booth had recovered sufficiently to resume his role in "The Apostate." "It was in this tragedy that Mr. Booth made such a hit on Tuesday," said the account. "His acting was so fearfully real in some of the scenes as to cause a thrilling sensation to pervade the audience, and when, at the conclusion of the play, in answer to the repeated calls for Mr. Booth, it was announced that he had seriously wounded himself, it seemed as though the climax of the tragedy had indeed been reached."

Meanwhile, up on Capitol Hill, the Legislature had been arguing over

Elmer Ellsworth of Mechanicville was loved by the Zoave Cadets and his President, Abraham Lincoln.

the arrangements for Lincoln's entertainment. Some legislators complained that Governor Morgan was trying to monopolize Lincoln during his stay, that he had invited the President-elect "to tuck himself under the Executive mahogany." It was pointed out that the Governor's dining room could seat only 24 people. Legislators, wishing to meet Lincoln, insisted on a grand banquet at the Delavan House, where the Lincolns would be staying. Still another big dinner was proposed at Congress Hall. It was finally agreed to prepare all three meals and let Lincoln make his own decision after his arrival. He chose the Governor's dinner, served "in the Russian style."

As the presidential train proceeded, section workers of the New York Central sounded every rail in the 298 miles of eastbound track. Meanwhile, Lincoln made speeches at the stops; they were in no way distinguished. Deliberately he avoided any statement of future policy and projected an attitude of humility. Repeatedly he said, with varied phrasings: "I appear mainly to see you and to let you see me and to bid you farewell"; or "I am not vain enough to believe that you are here from any wish to see me as an individual, but because I am for the time being the representative of the American people."

Farther south, another train was moving eastward, stopping frequently so its chief passenger could address the assembled masses. Jefferson Davis was making his way from his Mississippi plantation to Montgomery, Alabama, first capital of the newly declared Confederacy.

It became apparent as early as Cincinnati that Lincoln's stamina was not standing up well to the strain of frequent speechmaking and endless handshaking. His voice grew husky and he was troubled with a soreness in the chest. Word was telegraphed ahead to Albany that an anticipated gala demonstration by the Wide-Awakes would not be welcome. The Wide-Awakes (who are described in more detail in the chapter "Hopes Dashed") heeded the request.

After the train left Buffalo, it made brief stops at Batavia, Rochester, Clyde, Syracuse, Utica, Little Falls, Fonda, and Amsterdam. Lincoln had been showing himself along the route in what a reporter described as "a shocking bad hat and a very thin old overcoat." After passing Utica, Mrs. Lincoln took action. She whispered something to their black servant, William, who vanished momentarily and came back with a new hat and a fine broadcloth overcoat. "Since then," the newsman wrote, "Mr. Lincoln has looked 50 percent better." On the outskirts of Schenectady, a careless gunner touched off a cannon too close to the train as it passed. The concussion shattered several windows in the forward coach. Unperturbed, Lincoln spoke a few words from the rear platform in Schenectady.

When the train passed the West Albany car-shops at 2:20 p.m., a signal was flashed to the Dudley Observatory, and the measured firing of a 21-gun salute began. The train stopped at the Broadway crossing, where the reception committee awaited. But here a hitch occurred. The 25th Regiment, which was to provide military escort for the parade to the Capitol, had not yet arrived. A half-hour passed before it put in an appearance. The crowd grew impatient and there were shouts of "Show us the rail splitter!" "Trot out Old Abe!"

For Elmer Ellsworth, native of Mechanicville, this was a second triumphal homecoming within the year. His Chicago Zouaves had covered the same route on tour and had given performances in Albany and Troy.

Albany's Democratic mayor, George H. Thacher, rode with Lincoln in a barouche, heading a parade that came down Broadway and turned up State Street. A banner across Broadway shouted, "Welcome to the Capital of the Empire State—No More Compromise!" Never had the streets of Albany been so choked with humanity. People had poured into the city from a wide radius, even from New England. Lincoln stood up, bareheaded and waving, most of the way. A witness recalled: "I thought him the tallest man I ever saw and he did not seem homely to me."

A well-dressed man on the sidewalk audibly remarked: "The Negro-lover will never get to the Executive Mansion." A big burly fellow turned loose on him and gave him a bloody nose. In all probability, mingling in the throng, or standing at the window of his hotel room, J. Wilkes Booth was getting his first sight of the man he would one day murder.

Driven directly to the old Capitol, Lincoln was received by Governor Morgan, who led him out on the pillared portico to face a cheering throng. Here he spoke a few words which could be heard only by those nearest the steps. For the first time on the trip he publicly admitted his weariness. "I have neither the voice nor the strength to address you at any greater length," he said.

On the way to address the Legislature in the Assembly Chamber, Lincoln showed his sense of humor. There had been a recent flurry of graft charges against some legislators. Passing a table, Lincoln said with a sly grin: "I want to get rid of my hat—only for a time though. Shall I be safe in leaving it here?"

His humbleness was evident in the speech that followed: "It is with feelings of great diffidence, and I may say feelings of awe perhaps greater than I have recently experienced, that I meet you here in this place. The history of this great State, the renown of those great men that have stood here, and been heard from here, all crowd around my fancy, and incline me to shrink away from any attempt to address you. . . . It is true that while I hold myself, without mock modesty, the humblest of all individuals that have ever been elevated to the Presidency, I have a more difficult task to perform than any one of them."

Once more Lincoln shied away from any policy statement, saying: "When the time comes, I shall speak as well as I am able for the good of the present and future of this country—for the good both of the North and the South of this country." A round of applause followed this statement.

That same day Jefferson Davis was taking his oath of office as President of the Confederacy.

After dining with the Governor, the Lincolns returned to the Delavan House, only a block from Booth's Stanwix Hall, to a large reception, with prolonged handshaking. The legislators had their way, and Lincoln lost more rest.

The schedule called for the Lincoln party to leave Albany at 10 a.m. on Tuesday, but an ice-jam in the river forced a change in plans. There was as yet no bridge at Albany, and the Hudson River Railroad to New York was distinct from the New York Central. The normal practice was for through passengers to cross the river by ferry when it was open, on the ice when it was not, but the February freshet complicated matters, forcing the inaugural train to detour north to a bridge beyond Troy. This meant an earlier start than had been anticipated.

Lincoln felt "far from well" when he was awakened at 7 a.m. A half-hour later an escort headed by Mayor Thacher arrived at the hotel to accompany the presidential party to the train, and the bright uniformed Burgesses Corps marched in the van. Mrs. Lincoln and their three sons were making the most of the trip, enjoying its excitement. As the train moved north to Waterford Junction, crowds gathered at West Troy (Watervliet), Cohoes, Waterford, and Green Island to catch a glimpse of the new President. He smiled and waved.

Upon arriving at the Troy depot, Lincoln found a throng of 15,000 people waiting and an elevated platform for him to mount. Though he had not planned a stop, he could not disappoint them. He detrained and complimented them, saying: "Since I have left my home it has not been my fortune to meet an assemblage so compact and yet so good-natured as the one before which I now stand."

At Troy a fresh train was waiting with steam up. The locomotive, named the *Union,* pulled a lavish new parlor coach, built for the use of rail officials. Lined with crimson plush and hung with blue silk, the car was fitted out with Brussels carpet, ottomans, divans, and a hand-carved center table. Lincoln voiced a mild protest at its elegance as he boarded. Meanwhile, 600 employees of the Hudson River Railroad, working overtime, patrolled every segment of the track from Albany to New York. More crowds lined the right of way at East Albany, Greenbush, Stuyvesant, and Castleton. At Hudson, Lincoln consented to another brief talk. Cannon boomed as the train progressed, and skaters paced it on the river ice, waving flags and banners. More speech stops were made at Rhinebeck, Poughkeepsie, Fishkill, and Peekskill, and the train rolled into New York at 3 p.m. The official reception there was cool. Mayor Fernando Wood, a bitter opponent of Lincoln, had proposed the secession of New York City from the Union.

Although Senator William H. Seward would not take office as Secretary of State until the inauguration on March 4, he already was picking up the reins in Washington, and his son, Frederick, had left Albany to join him. During the overnight stop at Philadelphia, Frederick Seward came to Lincoln's hotel room with an urgent message from his father. The letter said that strong evidence of a plot to assassinate Lincoln while he was passing through Baltimore had been discovered, and begged him to alter the itinerary. This, coming on top of a similar warning he had been given by the detective, Allen Pinkerton, convinced Lincoln that he should not run the risk. Secretly, he left the main party at Harrisburg and completed the journey in a regular sleeping car that passed unnoticed through Baltimore in the dead of night.

On April 12 the guns spoke at Fort Sumter. Cooperstown native Captain Abner Doubleday (to be honored later as the "inventor" of baseball) fired the first Union cannons in reply to the bombardment. Henry Rathbone of Albany hastened home from abroad to enlist. Elmer Ellsworth, with Lincoln's influence, was commissioned a lieutenant of dragoons.

Meanwhile, Booth continued his engagement at the Gayety. Presently a Buffalo actress, Henrietta Irving, joined the stock company, taking a room at Stanwix Hall. On the night of April 26, she burst into Booth's room in a fit of jealousy, snatched up his dagger and slashed him on the forehead. She rushed back to her own room to make a gesture of suicide with the dagger. (She recovered and later married a Troy actor named Eddy.) Had Henrietta's aim been better—or her intent more earnest—she might have saved the life of Lincoln.

Adapted from *Times Union* articles: "Albany Gaily Greeted Lincoln in 1861," February 7, 1954; "Threads of Lincoln-Booth Tragedy First Crossed in Albany," February 12, 1961; "Lincoln Here: Tracks are Guarded," February 19, 1961.

1862

★ ★ ★ ★ ★ ★ ★ ★ ★ ★ ★ ★ ★ ★

The Race for the Monitor

EXCEPT FOR THAT Pearl Harbor Sabbath, the blackest date in the annals of the United States Navy befell on a Saturday—the 8th of March, 1862. That day the Confederacy unleashed its new and frightening weapon of the sea—the ironclad *Merrimac*. A dispatch clicking over wires from Fortress Monroe, Virginia, spread alarm verging on hysteria across the North—a stunning about-face from the elation engendered by Grant's recent capture of Forts Henry and Donelson.

The Albany *Argus* joined other papers to report: "The dullness of Old Point Comfort was startled today by the announcement that a suspicious looking vessel, supposed to be the *Merrimac,* looking like a submerged house with the roof only above water, was moving down from Norfolk. . . . There was nothing protruding above the water, except a flagstaff flying the rebel flag and a short smoke stack. . . . As soon as she came within range of the *Cumberland,* the latter opened on her with heavy guns, but the balls struck and glanced off, having no more effect than peas from a pop gun." The story described, with an obvious absence of real information, a confused melee that had ensued—Navy ships riddled, set afire, running aground—and left the outcome in doubt, concluding only that the dreadful raider had retired from the scene at nightfall, little damaged.

Readers knew that the very backbone of the federal Navy lay seemingly at the mercy of this bizarre craft. In Hampton Roads, like sitting ducks, were clustered 17 government warships mounting 222 guns all told, plus many charter vessels.

The shock wave that billowed up the Atlantic seaboard was comparable to the invasion panic of the Pacific Coast in the wake of Pearl Harbor. The "terrible engine of war"—a scuttled first-class frigate of the U.S. Navy which the rebels had salvaged and rechristened the

C.S.S. *Virginia*—was on the loose. They had since plated her with steel armor and now called her the *Merrimac*.

Lincoln called an emergency cabinet meeting that Sunday. The excitable Secretary of War, Edwin M. Stanton, was beside himself. He strode from room to room, waving his arms, lamenting that the *Merrimac* would no doubt polish off the rest of the fleet, then "come up the Potomac and disperse Congress, destroy the Capitol and public buildings; or she might go to New York and Boston and destroy those cities."

Stanton fired off telegrams to the Governors of New York, Massachusetts, and Maine, imploring them to gird up their defenses. General George B. McClellan wired the military commanders of six northern harbors to place their ports "in the best possible condition for defense, and do your best to stop her should she endeavor to run your batteries."

Of those harbors, the most critical to the Union was New York. Governor Edwin D. Morgan reacted to Stanton's message as if stung by a bee. He arranged for a special train to stand ready with steam up at East Albany to whisk him to New York in case the *Merrimac* moved north. He ordered all available volunteer regiments into the New York Harbor forts and put the state militia on alert. He readied the state's last-ditch plan to assemble all steamships, down to tugs and ferries, in the Upper Bay and send them swarming down upon the "monster" as a compact fleet, if she came, and "smother" her.

On the heels of the evil tidings from Virginia, however, came news that changed despair to joy. While smoke still hung upon the bloodied waters, a preposterous little machine crept into Hampton Roads and took shelter almost apologetically beside the grounded *Minnesota*. In her bowels, below the waterline, were a begrimed crew, weary and nauseated from the mere effort of keeping the object afloat in stormy ocean waves en route down the Jersey coast. The mystery craft, of course, was the *Monitor*—alias Ericsson's Folly, the iron pot, the tin can on a shingle, the Yankee cheesebox on a plank.

The *Merrimac* emerged again at dawn, snorting black smoke, to complete the carnage. The newcomer stood forth, a David against a Goliath, and checkmated the South's best gamble to break the blockade that was sure to strangle her in the end.

How the *Monitor* came to pivot upon that crucial pinpoint of history is a narrative of suspense, of happenstance, even of sheer luck, without which the North may not have won the Civil War. The pieces began to fall in place in early September, 1861. On that day, Cornelius H. (Harry) Delamater emerged from Willard's Hotel in Washington for an evening stroll. On the steps he met Cornelius S. Bushnell, a business acquaintance. Delamater was a spirited and witty Irish American, born in Rhinebeck, New York, who went to work in his teens for a Manhattan iron foundry and now, at the age of 40, owned the foundry. The other Cornelius was head of a Connecticut railroad and owned a shipyard at Mystic. Both were in Washington for the identical purpose—to secure war contracts.

Bushnell had that day clinched a contract for an armored gunboat, the *Galena*. One part of the proposal was bothering him. Some doubt had been cast upon the *Galena's* ability to carry the proposed weight of iron bars. He confided this to Delamater, who said he knew just the man to settle the quandary: Captain John Ericsson. Ericsson was an engineer, inventor, and something of a mathematical genius. Born in Sweden, he had lived in England for a time and come to New York in 1839. Now 58, he lived and worked alone in a graystone house at 95 Franklin Street. (His wife had joined him briefly in America, then returned to England because, as he said, "She was jealous of a steam engine.") A rugged, rather austere individual, he was not the type to make many friends. The closest one he had made this side of the Atlantic was Harry Delamater, whose iron works he had helped to success by giving it his experimental jobs.

To his friend Harry, Ericsson had shown a cardboard model of an iron "floating battery" he had invented but could get no one to build— a kind of elongated raft, imposed upon a smaller hull with a round gun-turret for superstructure to be rotated at will by a donkey engine. He also showed Delamater a gold medal and laudatory letter from Napoleon III in appreciation of Ericsson's having submitted the model as a possible aid against Russia during the Crimean War. Though the French emperor already was using some ironclads, he returned the model, and the inventor stowed it away on a shelf as "one of the hobbies of my lifetime," and went on to other things.

When the war broke out, Harry Delamater argued with John Ericsson into the small hours that he ought to offer the idea to the U.S. government as a matter of patriotism. Ericsson was willing it should be used in the Union cause but reluctant to make the overture because of an ancient grudge he nursed against the Navy Department. "All right, John," his friend persisted. "Then write a letter to President Lincoln." This Ericsson did, but received no reply. (It may be the letter never was mailed, or went astray.)

And so the box containing the model still reposed on its shelf the night Bushnell took the night train to New York. Ericsson studied

Bushnell's problem and advised him that the *Galena,* for all its iron, would be seaworthy. The visitor was reaching for his hat when Ericsson rather diffidently "inquired if I would not like to see and have a plan of an impregnable battery that could be built in 90 days, most likely in time to meet and destroy the *Merrimac.*" Bushnell pricked up his ears and watched his host bring the box from a cupboard, brushing dust from its cover. "It was less than ten minutes," Bushnell remembered, "before I fully awoke to the fact that salvation was in store for our government and country. And so I assured Ericsson. He turned the plans, box and all, over to me to handle just as I desired."

Guarding the shabby box as if it held diamonds, Bushnell sped to Hartford, where he knew Secretary of the Navy Gideon Welles was packing to move to Washington. Welles took one look and told Bushnell to return to Washington as fast as possible and show it to the naval board on ironclads.

On August 28, Bushnell had wired John F. Winslow and John A. Griswold, two iron manufacturers at Troy, asking if they would accompany him to Washington to help him sew up the *Galena* contract. Bushnell valued these men because their iron works were among the largest in the country, also because they and their silent partner, Congressman Erastus Corning, were men of prestige and power in the world of finance, and because they had important connections in government circles. Corning was, in fact, the founder and overlord of the two iron works in Troy.

Indicative of the behind-the-scenes role Corning would play in the unfolding drama was the letter Winslow wrote Corning on the day he was leaving Troy for Washington. Winslow informed the Congressman of his purpose to seek contracts for armor plate, adding significantly: "I would like you to send me a letter of introduction to Mr. Welles and say that any contract Griswold and I will undertake will be carried out. The contract will have to be made in the names of Griswold and myself as you happen to be a member of Congress and cannot appear as contractor with Government."

The Corning Papers in the Albany Institute of History and Art include a series of letters between Corning and Winslow in which the influence the Congressman could exert in high places, to facilitate the armor plate contracts, is a recurring theme.

Bushnell, cardboard box under his arm, rode all night on the train from Hartford. Arriving in Washington on a Sunday morning, he ordered a carriage and invited Messrs. Winslow and Griswold, who were still in the capital, to go for a drive with him in the suburbs. As the horses clip-clopped along, Bushnell offered his friends half-interest in the contract to build the "battery," providing such a contract could be had. He warned them there might be tough sledding because of Ericsson's disfavor among some high naval persons, dating from the unfortunate affair of the *Princeton,* the inventor's first screw-propeller boat, on which a gun had exploded with tragic results. Before the drive was ended, the trio had agreed upon a strategy: they would go right to the top, using their influence with Secretary of State Seward to win an audience with Lincoln.

When Secretary Seward opened his office the morning after the carriage ride, he found three impatient men. Seward was justifiably concerned that if the *Merrimac* did breach the Northern blockade, England and France might recognize the Confederacy, an event which would shift the balance of the war. Quickly persuaded, he gave them "a strong letter of introduction" to Lincoln. The President received them that same evening, saw what was in the box, and said, "I will meet you tomorrow at 10 o'clock at the office of Commodore Smith and we will talk it over."

By mutual consent, Winslow was spokesman of the group. He stayed up most of that night to prepare his case by studying Ericsson's plans. In the morning they met the three-man Naval Committee on Ironclads in the scantily furnished office of its senior officer, Commodore Joseph Smith. Lincoln sat cross-legged on an empty box. Winslow talked well enough to convince two members of the board, but the third held out, insisting the craft would be unstable. The session broke up with Lincoln's earthy remark: "Well, all I can say is what the fat girl said when she put her leg in the stocking—'It strikes me there's something in it.'"

No man was better qualified to answer the charge of instability than Ericsson, but it would take some doing to get him to plead his own cause. He had sworn never to step foot in Washington again. Bushnell entrained anew for New York. He first looked up Delamater, and together they rode to Ericsson's house. By insinuating that his plan was nearer acceptance than it was, they persuaded him to pocket his grudge. Once there, he learned that actually his proposal was being rejected on the score of instability. This angered the stubborn Scandinavian so that he launched into a masterful defense which won the board over. "Go home and start her immediately," Secretary Welles told him.

Ericsson hired a draftsman and began madly turning out detailed plans. Winslow and Griswold hurried back to Troy to tool up their plants for the iron plating. These three and Busnell joined in the so-called Battery Associates, or Ericsson Syndicate. Their aim was not just the one *Monitor,* but contracts for a future series of boats of that model. (Actually, they later won contracts for eight more.)

A note of urgency runs through the building of this nautical freak. Before the end of September, Winslow prodded Ericsson to rush him specifications for the plates "as I want to prepare the slabs in readiness for rolling." The industrialist in Troy and the engineer in New York kept needling one another for more speed. On October 8, Winslow wrote Ericsson: "I infer from the tone of your dispatches that you do not think us at this end fully up to the importance of pushing the delivery. Unless I err greatly in my calculations, you will receive iron from and after Monday at such a rate that you will cry, 'Hold in mercy.'"

The very workmen who labored in round-the-clock shifts at Troy and the Greenpoint section of Brooklyn seem to have sensed that the fate of the nation might hang upon their efforts. And the hardest worker of all was Ericsson himself, who was to be found at almost any hour of day or night in the shipyard, watchful of the smallest detail.

Ericsson altered his original plans as he went along, so the government did not get exactly the vessel for which it contracted; for example, he changed dimensions and reduced the weight of deck armor. He also conveniently forgot the contract stipulation for "masts, spars, sails, and rigging."

The rapid-fire organization that was whipped up to produce the *Monitor* under the pressure of great events was the classic example of American industrial know-how for its day. Its key man was Winslow of Troy. Griswold, as president of the Troy City Bank, served as the syndicate's treasurer, negotiating loans to meet payroll demands and the payment of sub-contractors.

Iron plates could not be rolled rapidly enough at the two Troy plants alone, so sub-contracts for these were farmed out to other companies. Most of the iron ore came down the Champlain Canal by barge for delivery at the riverside foundries in South Troy. Completed plates were then sent by river as long as the Hudson remained open, by rail when it froze.

Meanwhile, reports kept seeping north that the *Merrimac* was nearly ready for action, and public suspense mounted apace. Griswold wrote to Ericsson on January 10: "You cannot imagine the intense and almost agonizing anxiety of all the heads, from the President down, to have one boat to use."

A blanket of security was hung over the *Monitor*, but leaks occurred. Still, few people took it seriously. The *New York Times*, hammering away at the need for a good ironclad to send against the *Merrimac*, was probably referring obliquely to the Ericsson boat when it complained of "numerous charlatans who are allowed to palm their contrivances upon the public, at the public's cost, upon the simple indorsement of political wire-pullers."

The name, *Monitor*, was proposed by Ericsson himself, only ten days before the launching, in a letter to the assistant Navy secretary, Gustavus Vasa Fox, saying: "The impregnable and aggressive character of this structure will admonish the leaders of the Southern Rebellion."

Despite the secrecy, a respectable audience convened in a drizzling rain at the Greenpoint shipyard to watch the first all-iron ship swim or sink. Bets were made among the spectators as to whether or not she would dive to the bottom of the East River. Ericsson exhibited his own confidence by taking a stand on deck, toward the stern, in the center of an intrepid group. (As a precaution, a lifeboat was nearby.) As the *New York World* described the event:

"At ten minutes before 10 o'clock [on January 30, 1862], the braces were knocked away, and the vessel began to move slowly toward the water. The stars and stripes, floating from each end, began to flutter and to catch the breeze as she started. . . . Amidst the greatest anxiety on shore and on board, the vessel moved easily into the water, not immersing more than six feet of her forward deck, and sailed gracefully out into the stream for some distance. . . . The anxiety gave way to enthusiasm, and all cheered to the best of their ability, including, to their credit be it said, those who had lost money by bets on the certainty of her sinking."

The crew of 46 men and 12 officers, volunteers all, had been recruited from naval ships then in New York Harbor. Assigned to her command was Lieutenant John L. Worden, a bearded, 44-year-old Navy career man.

Unsung civilian heroes of the crew were some men from the Delamater Iron Works. They had built the boiler and engines and went along to nurse them, remaining on Harry Delamater's payroll the while.

The test runs were disheartening. The engines tended to run backward and the steering was unmanageable. Navy officials wanted to put her back in drydock to replace the rudder. Ericsson was furious. "The *Monitor* is mine," he protested. (Technically, he was right; the government had not yet paid for the ship.) "And I say it shall not be done. Put in a new rudder? They would waste a month in doing that.

I will make her steer just as easily in three days." And he did.

Delay followed delay. Assistant Navy Secretary Fox telegraphed again: "It is important that you should say exactly the day the *Monitor* can be at Hampton Roads."

Lieutenant Worden began the log of the U.S. Steamer *Monitor:* "Remarks, 25th February, 1862. Comes in with fine weather. At 3 o'clock P.M. received crew from Receiving Ship *North Carolina.* Vessel put in commission by Captain Almy. This day ends with clear cold weather."

On March 6, the watch entered these words: "At 10:30 A.M. left the Navy Yard. Crossed the bar and discharged the pilot at 4 P.M."

The Yankee cheesebox-on-a-raft was finally on the way to her rendezvous with destiny.

A few nights after the battle with the *Merrimac,* the entire labor forces of the Albany Iron Works and the Rensselaer Iron Works turned out for a torchlight parade in Troy. They fitted out a wagon as a float carrying a huge "illuminated transparency" of the battle. On the opposite side were portraits of Ericsson, Griswold, and Winslow. Beneath were the words: "Honor to whom honor is due." Below was a quote from General John Wool's telegram to Winslow: "The *Monitor* has saved everything inside and outside the fort."

Adapted from "Monitor Centennial Issue," *New York State and the Civil War,* January, 1962; and "Strange Battle: Monitor vs. Merrimac," *Times Union,* March 5, 1961.

1865

★ ★ ★ ★ ★ ★ ★ ★ ★ ★ ★ ★ ★ ★

Booth's Bullet

PRESIDENT LINCOLN dropped in at the War Department offices, as was his daily custom, the morning of April 14, 1865, and remarked to Secretary of War Edwin M. Stanton that General Grant had backed out of his engagement to accompany him and Mrs. Lincoln to Ford's Theater that evening. This was no great news to Stanton, who had been privately urging Grant not to go, and "if possible, to dissuade Lincoln from going."

Stanton's secret-service men had picked up rumors enough to suggest that it might be dangerous for the two great war leaders to appear in public together at that moment. (Grant had received Lee's surrender at Appomatox Court House on April 9.) Grant had agreed that the theater party was unwise, but he needed an excuse. Mrs. Grant was happy to oblige. It appears that she could not abide the company of Mary Todd Lincoln. Only a few days earlier, during a visit by the Lincolns to the General's headquarters at City Point, Virginia, Mrs. Grant had been acutely embarrassed when Mrs. Lincoln flew into a temper tantrum. Mrs. Grant told her husband he would have to get out of the date and gave him an alibi: she was going to visit their children in New Jersey, and Grant promised to follow her at once.

It was a last-minute thing, trying to find another couple. Stanton urged Lincoln at least to have a competent guard for company. "May I have your man Eckert?" Lincoln asked. "I have seen Eckert break five pokers, one after the other, over his arm." Major Thomas E. Eckert was a big, muscular man, who was in charge of the War Department's telegraph office. He had actually broken pokers, which had come in a shipment to the Department, to prove that they were made from a poor grade of iron. Stanton said he had special work for Eckert that night and could not spare him.

Meanwhile, Mrs. Lincoln scouted around and found someone. Clara Harris, aged 23, comely daughter of U.S. Senator Ira Harris from Albany, was known to the White House from social contacts. She had recently become engaged to Colonel Henry R. Rathbone, also of Albany, her step-brother. Rathbone, tall and courtly, was one of Albany's most eligible young men. His family and social connections were impressive. His late father, who left him a tidy fortune, had been Jared L. Rathbone, wholesale grocer, sometime mayor of the city, and president of Albany Medical College. Henry was a cousin of John F. Rathbone, who had grown so rich so fast with his stove factory that he retired at the age of 35.

After graduation from Union College in 1857, Henry Rathbone toyed with the study of law in an Albany office. But he had $200,000 and was foot-loose. In 1859, he shoved off to see Europe. He was still abroad when the Civil War erupted. The haste with which he sped home may be judged by the fact that he was commissioned a captain in the New York 12th Infantry on May 14, 1861. He was a brilliant success in the military, and was breveted Major for gallant and meritorious service in battles of the campaign from the Rapidan to Petersburg, Virginia. Once he lay wounded for 48 hours among the littered dead on a battlefield. Later he was attached to the office of Provost Marshal and was breveted a full colonel in March, 1865, though only 28 years of age, for meritorious service in organizing volunteer armies.

The betrothed couple were only too happy at the honor of being invited to accompany the President and his lady. While this problem was being resolved, John Wilkes Booth was nosing about Ford's Theater, with special attention to the presidential box. This he could do with impunity, being well known to the theater staff from having performed there in times past. Indeed, he had played on Ford's stage as recently as March 18, as Pescara in "The Apostate," the same play he had been acting in Albany in February, 1861, when Lincoln passed through. This proved to be the last theatrical performance he ever gave.

It was after 8 o'clock when the President and Mrs. Lincoln got into their carriage at the White House. Lincoln had been busy at his desk. The play would be well under way before they reached the theater, but no matter. The coachman drove around by way of H Street to pick up Miss Harris and her fiancé at the home of Senator Harris. Colonel Rathbone was not in uniform, nor was he armed.

A rustle swept the audience as the foursome entered the box. A rocking-chair had been placed, as was customary, for the President. As the play went on, Lincoln, observing that the young couple were holding hands, grasped his wife's hand for a tender moment in the semi-darkness. No one noticed that the policeman on guard in the corridor behind the box had stepped out and gone to have a quick drink at a nearby saloon.

A few minutes past 10, Booth softly opened the door and slipped into the box. He held a small derringer pistol with only one bullet in its chamber. He pointed it at the back of the President's head and pulled the trigger. For a long moment no one reacted. Booth dropped the pistol, pulled out a knife, and pushed to the front of the box, intending to vault its railing. Rathbone jumped up and grappled with him. Booth's knife flashed and cut Rathbone's arm to the bone. The action on stage was suddenly stilled.

Booth, always agile, dropped from the box about ten feet to the stage. In the leap, one foot caught in the draped flag, and the other foot, taking the brunt of the fall, gave way. The bone had broken just above the instep. Booth hopped across the stage, making for an exit. "Stop him!" Rathbone shouted. Nobody did. There is some confusion as to exactly what Booth said at this point—"Sic semper tyrannis!" or "Revenge for the South!" At any rate, the actor did not speak his line loudly enough to be heard by the audience. In the alley behind the theater, he mounted a waiting horse and galloped away.

Mrs. Lincoln glanced around at her husband. His head had fallen forward, chin on chest. She screamed. Clara Harris leaned over the coping of the box and pleaded: "Water! Somebody please bring water." Rathbone, with blood flowing down his arm, dashed into the narrow corridor. He found the entry door from the dress circle propped shut from within by a wooden bar which Booth had placed. He pulled the bar away to admit Dr. Charles Leale, a physician who had been in the audience.

When the stricken President was carried to a home across the street, Rathbone followed with the two women. He sat with them in the parlor while Miss Harris stroked the hands of the hysterical Mrs. Lincoln. After a time, Rathbone slowly toppled to the floor, faint from loss of blood. He was two months recovering.

A wild rumor was soon flying that Secretary Seward had been assassinated, too. At almost the identical time when Booth fired the shot, one of his accomplices, Lewis Paine, gained entry to the Seward home under the pretense that he had been sent with medicine from Seward's physician. He insisted he must deliver it in person to the patient. Only nine days before, Seward had been severely injured in trying to stop his runaway horses while out for a drive. His lower jaw and an arm were broken, and he had a brain concussion. With a steel brace on his jaw and his arm immobilized, he was an invalid in an upstairs room. As Paine mounted the stairs, Seward's son, Frederick, emerged on the landing in a dressing-gown to see what was causing the commotion. By virtue of his father's injury, Frederick Seward was now Acting Secretary of State. He told the intruder that the patient was asleep and could not be disturbed, adding, "I must say you are a very strange messenger for Dr. Verdi to have employed."

Paine now aimed a pistol at Fred Seward and pulled the trigger. The gun missed fire. Turning it into a bludgeon, Paine beat young Seward with its butt until he slumped to the floor, his skull fractured. Paine whipped out a bowie knife, burst into Secretary Seward's room, and slashed away at the head and shoulders of the helpless figure in the bed. The metal brace on Seward's jaw deflected the blows and thus saved his life. He was frightfully cut about the face and neck and lay at death's door for two more weeks from shock and loss of blood. The assailant was pulled off by others of the household and finally fled, leaving behind a scene of carnage. He had wounded five people in the Seward home, though none fatally. Outside, David Herold, who had been holding Paine's horse, became alarmed at cries of "Murder!" and galloped off and joined Booth in his flight.

Another Booth accomplice, George Atzerot, assigned to kill Vice-President Andrew Johnson, lost his nerve and got drunk instead.

A spark of life remained in Lincoln all during the night. Shortly after 7 o'clock in the morning of the 15th he passed away. Secretary of War Stanton spoke to the silent room: "Now he belongs to the ages."

On Saturday morning, the words of Governor Reuben E. Fenton opened the legislative session in Albany: "It becomes my painful duty to announce to the Legislature the death of Abraham Lincoln, President of the United States. It is with emotions of profound sorrow that I make this announcement to your honorable body. Such an event is a national calamity, and under the circumstances attending this bereavement, the nation weeps with heightened anguish. I have also to communicate to you the sad intelligence that our noble Secretary of State, an honored and favored son of New York, William H. Seward, was likewise the victim of the tragic plot of the assassins and now lies in an unconscious condition. May God spare his life to the nation."

Albany, like the rest of the nation, was stunned and incredulous at the news to which it awakened that day before Easter. The streets filled rapidly, and people clustered around newspaper bulletin boards, talking

Leslie's Illustrated *depicted Booth taking aim at Lincoln.*

in hushed tones and hungrily awaiting more information. Details of the tragedy were still vague and confusing. Belief came hard. Five days previously, these same streets had been wild with celebration of Lee's surrender. Jubilation had gone on all night long, with great bonfires, bells pealing, cannon booming, fireworks popping, and men shouting themselves hoarse with joy. Just yesterday these people had thrilled afresh at the news of Major General Robert Anderson's running up the Stars and Stripes again at Fort Sumter, exactly four years from the day he had lowered it. They thought they were through with bloodshed—and now this.

The paroxysm of public grief was spontaneous, deep, and genuine. There had been no time for propaganda to stir it up. The surge of sorrow grew because the people loved the man who was dead, as they had never before grown to love a chief of state. He had saved their nation and had won their love while doing it. Moreover, this was the first time a President of the United States had been murdered. The grief was all the more poignant because it struck on the eve of the first peaceful Easter in four years. Churches and cathedrals were prepared for glad hosannas. To the devout, it seemed that the risen Christ was crucified anew. Flags were half-masted. Buildings everywhere, including private homes, were draped in mourning. Drygoods stores soon sold out of black cloth. "Every countenance wore a look of sorrow," a news account reported.

With the grief flamed a quick, hot anger. In Troy, a stranger, D. L. Hunt of Rochester, stood reading a bulletin in front of the telegraph office, and reportedly said: "He ought to have been assassinated four years ago." A bystander called him a villain. Hunt struck him and ran down River Street, pursued by a mob. The posse caught him, got a rope around his neck and were about to hang him from a lamppost when a policeman intervened. The man was charged with assault and battery and clapped in jail for his own safety. In Lansingburgh, a milk peddler was heard to say, "Damn him, it is good enough for him." Someone started for a rope. The milkman whipped up his horse and got rapidly out of the neighborhood. In Saratoga a Southern girl was expelled from a female seminary for remarking: "Saturday was the happiest day of my life."

During the war, the Albany *Atlas and Argus* had been so outspoken against Lincoln's policies that at one period it had been barred from the mails as seditious. Now the paper ran an editorial saying: "It is impossible to conceal the fact that public sentiment is embittered toward the South by the recent crime committed in its name. The general amnesty contemplated by the late President was regarded as an act of magnanimity—as something more than Mercy, less than Justice. Yet the people were disposed to confirm it. . . . But when the response is the assassin's bullet and knife, when the dispenser of Mercy becomes the victim of vengeance, the public sentiment recoils. It no longer talks of pardon, of justice, even, but of revenge. . . . Yet if good men and true patriots will now appeal to the reason of the masses, and direct the government of the country in the calm consciousness of strength, the nation will be saved from the danger of its own passions."

The clergy, prepared to deliver sermons of rejoicing in the Easter liturgy, had to change the theme. Dr. William Sprague at Second Presbyterian Church said: "If we fail to carry out Lincoln's purposes, will not our sorrowful utterances in view of his death, nay will not the very mourning in which we have draped this place of our solemnities, bear testimony against us?" In some of the sermons a hardened attitude toward the South was plain. Still others saw in Booth's crime the curious workings of God's will. The Rev. Edgar Buckingham, at Troy's Unitarian Church, reasoned thus: "Mr. Lincoln's work on earth was done. . . . His work can never be undone. The nation is safe. Possibly it is safer than in the continuance of his life. . . . He was gentle. He was lenient; was he weak in tenderness?. . . . Possibly, the interest of the nation may be safer in the hands of a less forgiving man. Possibly we need the sternness of another mind, which will less readily believe in the possibility of conciliating the perjured and malignant, a man who will entertain a juster fear of the demoniacal spirit which the rebel leaders have shown."

The thoughts of the black congregations, as represented by the Rev. Jacob Thomas of the A. M. E. Zion Church in Troy, were particularly moving: "We, as a people, feel more than all others that we are bereaved. We had learned to love Mr. Lincoln as we have never loved man before. We idolized his very name. . . . To us as a despised people, he was a second Moses. . . . May God protect us and keep us from farther evils."

The Rev. David Dyer, chaplain at the Albany Penitentiary (used during the war to hold "offenders against the government"), told his listeners that the assassination was "the culmination of wickedness, party violence, and enmity. . . . This hellish spirit has branded our beloved President as a tyrant, and has planned and accomplished his death. I cannot forbear the conviction that the Confederate actors in this malignant plot have killed the best friend of the citizens of the Southern states."

By Sunday, Seward had regained consciousness but was unable to speak. He wrote on a pad: "Why doesn't the President come to see me? Where is Frederick? What is the matter with him?" Secretary of War Stanton was chosen to tell Seward the truth. Meanwhile, John Wilkes Booth was still at large and being reported "seen" in various cities. In Troy, a man named John Sweeney was arrested on suspicion of being Booth.

Wednesday, the 19th, was set for the White House funeral, after which the remains were to lie in state in the U.S. Capitol. The Mayor of Albany, Eli Perry, proclaimed simultaneous observances in his city, with closed stores, open churches, minute-guns, and tolling bells. Once it had been determined that burial would take place in Springfield, a clamor arose from northern cities to be allowed a final glimpse of the dead President. The route was changed to have the train retrace essentially the itinerary by which Lincoln had traveled to Washington in 1861. Thereupon the New York Legislature appointed a committee of three from the Senate, five from the Assembly, to meet the train in New York and accompany it across the state.

A deluxe car had been built for the use of Lincoln and other high officials on U.S. military railroads. This was now converted into the funeral coach. It was of a "deep chocolate" color. Heavy crepe festoons extended its length over the outside windows. The interior was hung with black tapestry, relieved by silver stars and tassels. Lincoln's coffin rested toward the rear. At the front end of the coach was a smaller casket—that of young Willie Lincoln, who had recently died in the White House and had been disinterred to go back home with his father. The train counted nine coaches. Its speed was a sedate 20 miles per hour, and all other traffic on a division was reduced to that during its transit. A pilot engine ran 10 minutes ahead to test the track. The distraught Mrs. Lincoln and her remaining two sons, Robert and Tod, were spared the ordeal of the funeral train. They went direct to Springfield.

The coffin was open to public gaze in New York's City Hall for 24 hours, April 24–5, while the train was switched to the Hudson River Railroad. Governor Fenton, Lieutenant Governor Thomas G. Alvord, and the legislative committee joined the cortege in New York to escort the remains to Albany. Many other ranking government and political figures rode the train. The slow, mournful progress up the river began Tuesday afternoon. Crowds silent and tearful gathered beside the tracks and at way stations. After night fell, bonfires blazed on the uplands. The same two locomotives that drew the inaugural train from Albany to New York in 1861 now served the funeral train. The *Constitution* moved ahead as pilot engine; the *Union* hauled the train. The bells of both engines were muffled. The *Union* was camouflaged with masses of crepe, streamers, and white rosettes. A flag bearing the word "Union" rode on the cowcatcher, rows of small American flags lined the railings, and a funeral wreath encircled the headlamp. The cab was festooned with black and white ribbons, and on either side, below the window, hung a portrait of the slain President.

As the train pulled into the East Albany station at 11 p.m., church bells tolled in unison and cannon boomed from the heights. A ferryboat bore the casket across the river in a weird, appropriate silence. Waiting at the Maiden Lane ferry landing stood the entire State Legislature and the Albany City Council headed by Mayor Perry. The coffin was laid gently upon a black hearse drawn by four white horses which bore it up to the old Capitol, followed by a solemn procession. Marching with the military were 100 city firemen with flaring torches. Seats and desks had been cleared from the Assembly Chamber. Beneath the great chandelier, a black catafalque, lined with white satin and fitted with silver mountings and a gold eagle, was prepared. The wall behind the Speaker's chair bore a placard with Lincoln's words: "I have the most solemn oath registered in Heaven to preserve, protect, and defend the government."

The casket was reverentially lowered onto the catafalque. At 1:15 in the morning, the lid was raised and a double row of mourners began to walk silently past. The lines moved at the rate of 60 to 70 people a minute. It was estimated that 50,000 persons looked upon the still, gaunt face of Lincoln in Albany.

Few residents slept that night. Many visitors really had no place to sleep. The hotels were overcrowded. Restaurants and places of public assembly remained open all night, and people roamed the streets. One group stayed in a school. Soldiers guarded the Capitol, and the watch at the casket was changed periodically. The militia guard was under the command of Brigadier General John F. Rathbone, the cousin of Colonel Henry Rathbone.

The lines of mourners extended all the way down the hill and around the corner on Broadway. A youth of 17, Andrew S. Draper, shinnied up a tree near the Capitol to see the arrival of the hearse. Four years before he had followed the cavalcade when Lincoln visited the same Capitol in life. This time he joined a line and passed the coffin once. Then he ran down the hill to stand in line and pass by a second time. When it was nearing 5 a.m., Andy ran all the way home and awakened his parents, saying, "It's time!" They arose and dressed, and the boy accompanied them through the line to gaze upon Lincoln for the third time. (Draper was to become New York State's first Commissioner of Education.)

By daylight, excursion trains and steamboats brought more visitors to town. On all sides they saw store windows displaying signs: "With malice toward none, with charity for all." "Let us resolve that the martyred dead shall not have died in vain." "And the victory that day was turned into mourning unto all the people."

When the coffin was closed at 12:30 p.m., thousands were still in line, disappointed. But the train had to move on.

Even while this scene was being enacted in Albany, an army search unit surrounded an old tobacco barn in Virginia. Hiding inside were John Wilkes Booth and his jittery young disciple, Davy Herold. When Booth, who was armed with a carbine, refused to come out, the shed was set afire. Herold surrendered. Whether Booth would have followed will never be known. A soldier, sighting Booth through one of the wide cracks which let in air for the drying of tobacco, disobeyed orders and shot Booth in the back of the neck. The assassin died a few hours later. The offending soldier was placed under arrest, but the public made such a hero of him that he was released and later was paid a share of the reward money. This man was Sergeant "Boston" Corbett; he had grown up in Troy and worked as a hatmaker in Albany.

Another procession escorted Lincoln's hearse from the Capitol to the funeral car. The train had been transferred meanwhile up to the North Troy bridge and around, and now stood at the Broadway crossing just above Lumber Street (Livingston Avenue). It pulled out for the west promptly at 4 p.m. on Wednesday, April 26.

Tried by a military commission, four of Booth's accomplices were hanged in Washington on July 7. Four others—Dr. Samuel Mudd, Edward Spangler, Samuel Arnold, and Michael O'Laughlin—were sentenced to imprisonment at hard labor in the Albany Penitentiary. News dispatches reported the four prisoners would be entrained for Albany almost at once. Local newspapers watched for their arrival in vain. Secretary of War Stanton, wanting them in a prison of greater security, had committed them instead to Fort Jefferson, on one of the Dry Tortugas Islands off Florida. McLaughlin died there of yellow fever. The other three were pardoned by President Andrew Johnson in 1869.

Senator Ira Harris ended his Washington career in 1867, accepted a professorship at Albany Law School, and retired to a farm he owned in Loudonville. With him returned his daughter, Clara, who had functioned so well as her father's hostess in Washington that the press described her as a "brilliant ornament to the society of Washington." That summer, she and the dashing Colonel Rathbone were wed in Albany. They set up housekeeping briefly in the family home he had inherited at 28 Eagle Street. Then they moved to a handsome house in Washington. They had three children and were recognized as a happy and devoted couple.

But a shadow hovered over their lives, and it darkened. Rathbone fell victim to spells of depression verging on melancholia. Friends said he brooded over that night in the box at Ford's Theater—that he blamed himself for not having been more alert. As the years passed, he also grew irrationally jealous of his wife; he could not tolerate having another man pay her notice, and was even jealous of her attentions to the children.

Rathbone resigned his commission in 1870 and thenceforth had no occupation. In 1876, they moved to Europe, ostensibly for the purpose of educating the children. They established a home in Hanover, Germany. Prolonged attempts were made to get him appointment in the consular service. The State Department today has 62 pages of letters recommending him for such a post, but, for reasons unknown, he never obtained it.

The last time the Rathbones were in Albany was on a visit in 1882. They summered at the old Harris farm in Loudonville, where Rathbone devoted three hours daily to reading history to his sons. There were strong indications then of family discord. Relatives later said that Clara had told them of Henry's fits of temper and jealousy; also that he was subject to dyspepsia "in its most aggravated form;" and that he had even once threatened her life. She discussed the question of a separation or divorce, but ruled it out because of the children. In the end, she agreed to return to Germany on condition that her sister, Louise Harris, would accompany them. A nurse for the children already was an established member of the household.

People in Albany subsequently recalled that Rathbone had "looked ill" during the visit, and some said they had feared for his sanity. The Colonel always kept firearms in the house, taking pride in his marksmanship. On the day before Christmas, 1883, he arose very early and started for the nursery. To reach it, he had to grope his way through the nurse's room. She awakened. Clara Rathbone got up and followed her husband, obviously agitated. She closed the nursery door and asked the nurse to guard it while she led her husband back to their bedroom.

Presently cries for help, followed by gunshots, issued from the bedroom. Louise Harris and the servant found the door locked, broke it in, and were confronted by a gory scene. Mrs. Rathbone lay across the bed, dying from bullet wounds in the breast. Her husband was sprawled on the floor bleeding from five self-inflicted dagger wounds.

A headline in an Albany paper on December 26 noted: "Albany Society Receives a Shock." The tragedy touching the Harris and Rathbone families created a sensation in the area for weeks. Rathbone recovered from his suicidal attempt and was brought to trial in Hanover late in January, 1884. He professed to have no memory of killing his wife, thinking an intruder did it. The German court stopped the trial when evidence was submitted that he had "shown signs of insanity at various times since Lincoln's death." He was committed to a private asylum for the insane in Germany and there spent the remainder of his many days, living until 1911.

A brother of Mrs. Rathbone, Colonel W. H. Harris, went abroad and took charge of the children, two boys and a girl. He raised them in Cleveland. One son, Henry Riggs Rathbone, later practiced law in Chicago and was elected to Congress.

Some 20 years passed. Shortly after the turn of the century, Mr. and Mrs. Charles E. McElroy rented a summer home in Loudonville, the old farmhouse of Senator Ira Harris, since owned by another daughter, Pauline, who lived in the city. Mrs. McElroy found its interior somewhat rundown and obtained permission to redecorate the dining-room. She already knew there was a walk-in closet off this dining-room. Its door, flush with the walls without wainscoting, had been papered over but could be opened.

Before the paperhangers came, Mrs. McElroy decided to see what was on the closet shelves. One thing she found was a folded old dress of the hoopskirt era—obviously once a fancy ballroom gown. It was of pink satin, though the pink had faded almost to white. Down the front of the skirt was a great blotch of rusty brown. Mrs. McElroy concluded the spot was blood. Her first thought was that a murder had sometime been committed in the house. She summoned others to look at it. "I never took the dress down," Mrs. McElroy said. "Frankly, I was scared to death because of the blood on it and didn't want to touch it."

Leaving the dress on the shelf, Mrs. McElroy had the closet door papered over to match the rest of the dining-room, and her family continued to rent the house for several summers. Only gradually, as she mentioned the dress among friends, did the legend start that this was the gown worn by Clara Harris the night of Lincoln's assassination, and that the brown spot was Lincoln's blood. The spot never was scientifically identified as human blood. If it was, it could not very well have been Lincoln's. Miss Harris was not near Lincoln in the box; Mrs. Lincoln had sat between them. Lincoln's head merely sank upon his chest, as if he had fallen asleep in his rocker, and his wound was not of the type that bled severely.

If it was Clara's dress, and if the spot was blood, it is more likely that it was Colonel Rathbone's blood. He was bleeding copiously from the knife wound in his arm, and he had sat next to his fiancée. What became of the dress? Nobody knows. The flourishing Albany legend to which it gave rise has several variations. One is that Mrs. McElroy burned it, along with rubbish she found in the house. (Mrs. McElroy firmly denied this.) Another version says that the son of the Rathbones, Henry, the Chicago attorney, was told of it, came East to look at it, and ordered it burned.

One thing is certain: the house in Loudonville no longer has the closet or the dress. The house, purchased by new owners just prior to World War I, was moved and altered. During the alterations, the dining-room storage closet was removed. The house stands now on Cherry Tree Lane.

Adapted from *Times Union* articles: "Threads of Lincoln-Booth Tragedy Crossed First in Albany," February 12, 1961; "A Tragedy That Blighted 2 More Lives," April 16, 1961.

PART TWO
★ ★ ★ ★ ★ ★ ★ ★ ★ ★ ★ ★ ★ ★

Set Changes

Downtown Albany

As ELKANAH WATSON was stepping briskly down State Street just after a heavy shower, he met two Dutch housewives in front of their stoops angrily sweeping mud off the walk.

"Here comes that infernal paving Yankee!" snorted one.

By mutual consent, they charged, with broomsticks menacingly upraised. Watson prudently retreated.

State Street had just been paved for the first time, its grade lifted so that rainwater, because there were no curbs, would run onto the flagstone walks. The burghers resented such alterations in their placid scheme of life, and Elkanah Watson personified the change that was engulfing them.

Well-traveled and forward thinking, Watson had arrived with the influx of New Englanders who began coming in the late 1700s, bringing energetic new ideas and unfamiliar customs to a town old and set in its ways—a Rip Van Winkle town that was "a world of queer old women, beds-in-the-wall, quack doctors, great tomes, smokers, eaters, drinkers, merry parties, herds of cattle, muddy streets piled with garbage, wandering pigs, and quaint houses."

Albany, so to speak, has lived two lives, with the Revolution as the dividing line. The place existed almost as many years prior to the Battle of Saratoga as it has since. The pristine Albany was essentially a medieval European town transplanted to American soil—as Quebec, for example, is to this day. Even the dogs (so the saying went) barked in Dutch. It was, perhaps more accurately, a curious hybrid of imported Holland town, frontier outpost, and military fortress.

Then the curtain fell, and rose again. The wooden village, as if by magic, had become a city of stone and brick. The sleepy provincial town was now a center of bustle and quick fortunes.

The downtown business heart of the new Albany coincided in almost identical extent with what was the total circumference of the old Albany. The boundaries of Dorpe Beverwyck—at the age when howl of wolf and scream of wildcat sounded outside the window and rattlesnakes coiled on Capitol Hill—were these: the Hudson River to the east, Hudson Avenue to the south, Lodge Street to the west, and Steuben Street to the north. (Some time later the stockade pushed south to Hamilton Street and north to Orange and Van Tromp Streets.)

In the great metamorphosis, certain individuals stand out most sharply: Elkanah Watson and Philip Hooker, of old; DeWitt Clinton and Erastus Corning, at midway; and Marcus T. Reynolds and John Boyd Thacher 2nd in more recent times. Watson, as a progressive stranger from Providence in 1789, took a good look around the town of which a French duke wrote: "I almost incline to think the young people here are old born." Watson decided it could stand remodeling. The streets were deplorable, so he instigated the paving. The eavesspouts were a nuisance. They copied those in Holland where runoff was directed into the canals by elongated spouts. In Albany, which had no canals, the system succeeded only in splashing passersby, so Watson had them sawed off. The Dutch townsfolk, thinking to neutralize him, elected him constable. This just gave him more incentive. He took to chasing pigs off the streets. He got an ordinance on the books prohibiting swine from roaming at will. This crusade especially irritated the inhabitants, accustomed to dumping their garbage on the streets and letting the pigs run as scavengers. If pigs were corralled, they argued, then they would have to pay someone to collect garbage. Yet there was nothing so clean as the scrubbed inside of a Dutch home.

Motorists who admire the splendid width of State Street may be interested to know that its girth was originally planned to protect the people from Indian attack. When, in 1654, the old Dutch Church parted company with the fort which was at the foot of Madison Avenue, and moved upstream to where State and Broadway come together (bringing the main settlement in its train), the church building functioned as much as a block-house as a church. The menfolk carried their firearms to worship and took seats handy to the loopholes. The church-blockhouse was purposely placed in the middle of the intersection so as to command a clean sweep of both approaches, in case the muskets were needed.

For this reason, State Street—originally a narrow Indian defile through the forest—grew inordinately wide. Later public structures, such as the market and the first English church (St. Peter's), followed the precedent and were built in the middle of Jonckers Street as it climbed the slope. Thus the street became a broad concourse, a convenience for the pioneers when the great western trek began.

Whether known as Fort Orange, or The Fuyck, or Beverwyck, or Willemstadt, Albany was a town under arms until after the Revolution. Its fort was the central institution. Actually, there was a sequence of four forts:

Fort Nassau—On Castle Island in the river, soon flooded and rebuilt on a hillside near the Normanskill. (This is described in more detail in the chapter, "Enter the Europeans.")

Fort Orange—On the riverbank near the Dunn Memorial Bridge, once described as "a miserable little fort built of logs, banked with earth inside, and armed with four or five small cannon."

Fort Albany—Erected by the British conquerors half-way up State Street hill (just above Lodge Street) in 1676, when the rampaging of King Philip's Indians across New England set the townspeople in a panic.

Fort Frederick—As Fort Albany was rechristened (in honor of a scion of the German house of Hanover, then holding the throne of England), when it had been stoutly and imposingly reconstructed with stone in 1735.

With the Union Jack whipping proudly over its bastions, Fort Frederick looked down protectively upon State Street until the United States of America was born. It was demolished in 1784 and its stones given to churches during that revulsion against all things British which also eventuated in the changing of street names: King Street to Lion (now Washington); Queen to Elk; Prince to Deer (now upper State); Duke to Eagle; Howe to Fox (now Sheridan); Johnson to Lark.

The city did not really start growing outside the limits defined by the stockade until around 1800. Only its burial-ground and the so-called "Indian Houses" (shelters for Indians who came with furs) had been outside the gates. The palisades (when 560 new ones were requisitioned in 1693) were 20 feet long and 12 inches wide, "of good smooth-barked pyne, not of your black-barked pyne."

The little Dutch town remained more or less impervious to British influence. Until long after the English were in possession, the first-comers persisted in calling it "The Fuyck" (a word now generally conceded to have referred to a funnel-shaped type of fish-net, likened to the flaring street northward from the Dutch church, to allow a wide angle of fire in case of enemy approach).

But the Yankee influence was less resistible. After the Revolution

Elkanah Watson, the "infernal paving Yankee," faced obstacles head-on and won.

there was a restless stirring. Enterprise was in the air with liberty. But Albany was still, for some time, a quiet city, a "perfect jewel of antiquity." Indeed, when the mayor once violated his own ordinance against galloping a horse through the streets in order to help put out a fire, he contritely paid his fine to the justice the next day.

Came Elkanah Watson, and more of his ilk, and the boom was on. Philip Hooker, too, had come from New England as a boy. He learned his father's trade of carpentry and rounded out into what may be called a practical architect. More than any other man, Philip Hooker was responsible for the 19th century semblance of Albany.

The fairytale Dutch buildings, with their high-ridged roofs and "step" gables facing the street, vanished utterly. It is lamentable no one had the foresight to save at least one of them. (Quackenbush House, of a less embellished style, was built in 1730 and almost lost to the city. Restoration efforts linked to the nation's Bicentennial in 1976 reclaimed it.) New England Renaissance took over, with Hooker at the helm. Indeed, Hooker helped to create, right here in Albany, a style of "American classicism."

Hooker practiced on churches, getting to be the ecclesiastical architect of the locality. His earliest known and still most famous work was the old Dutch Reformed Church, dated 1798, whose twin towers remain the most picturesque landmark of Pearl Street. (The rest of the church as spoiled, from the aesthetic viewpoint, by later alterations.)

Hooker's handiwork spread over Albany and to other cities. Virtually every public building in town was his, and many private dwellings as well. He designed the first State Capitol and the first City Hall (unless one counts the defunct Stadt Huys). He designed two theaters and a couple of banks, public markets, and, of course, the Albany Academy.

We have precious little of Hooker left: the Dutch Church steeples and the street-level front of the State Bank of Albany (now Norstar Bank) on State Street, and—the only complete building preserved—the Academy, now the Joseph Henry Memorial.

Hooker was destined to leave another indelible mark on downtown. Having been appointed city superintendent, he started the grading of the city's unfortunate hills and deep gullies. As the Patroon's people found it, and as it had remained past 1800, the Albany landscape consisted of narrow flats along the river hemmed in by a sharply rising 200-foot acclivity immediately behind. The river had sunk itself into the soft clay and gravel bottom left by glacial Lake Albany, and the sidestreams had been slashing into the edges ever since. Three distinct ridges thrust down toward the river. The center ridge became the community's backbone, State Street. The northern ridge defines Arbor Hill, and the southern ridge, considerably reduced, supports Madison Avenue.

The ravines between the ridges were deep, with brawling streams in their beds—the Foxenkill on the north and the Ruttenkill on the south. Today these creeks are imprisoned in underground sewers. Where the Foxenkill ran is now Sheridan Avenue. That gully, never filled, formerly sheltered "Gander Bay," a colony of rough-and-tough Irish foundrymen and their families. In subsequent years the Hawk Street viaduct (now gone) spanned the ravine.

The old Ruttenkill gorge was a real dilemma to the city, cutting back beyond Lark Street, 50 feel deep and 300 feet wide. It was occupied by brick-kilns, foul reservoirs, and rats. The name meant rat creek. There was even a gallows in the Ruttenkill ravine, and the last execution in the city took place there in 1827 when Jesse Strang, celebrated murderer of John Whipple at Cherry Hill, met his fate. More than 30,000 people flocked into town to see the trap dropped.

Philip Hooker studied the Albany scene and made recommendations for better street levels, including the honing down of State Street, which was more precipitous by far than now, with a grade of seven feet in 100. But even he despaired of leveling off the ravines for any cross streets.

He left that to Erastus Corning, who had broken into the hardware business in Troy. Corning moved into Albany in 1822, developed an iron industry, helped promote the first railroad, and became mayor. Bent upon the physical improvement of the town, he pushed the leveling of streets from where Hooker left off, and even tackled the pestiferous Ruttenkill. The dismal and unsanitary ravine was filled in a three-year project (1844–1847) employing 60 teams and 250 men who peeled down the Madison Avenue hill to plug it.

Water was another problem. At first there were wells, public and private. But the water was unpleasant and peppered with insects. So springs were tapped on the hill and wooden logs with holes bored through them were laid to carry the water down. Still many people preferred river water, even when it was muddy. Ultimately a reservoir was constructed on the present site of the Albany County Courthouse and water was piped into it from the back-country streams.

During its adolescence, the town suffered from three recurrent catastrophes: plagues, floods, and fire. The disease epidemics were veritable scourges—cholera, smallpox, and typhus. Great numbers would fall ill in such outbreaks, and many would die.

The spring freshets posed a particular problem. Broadway, earlier known as Market Street, was the main business thoroughfare, while Pearl Street remained largely residential. The floods, getting increasingly out of hand as the timber was stripped from the Adirondacks and spring runoff grew more tremendous, forced stores to move higher. Thus Pearl Street became a mercantile artery.

Fires also modified the city. They came with distressing frequency, and when they started among the close-packed wooden buildings with only primitive protection, the town was easy prey. Even a small fire was apt to spread and create a large black gap, sometimes blocks in extent. One blaze in the 1790s, for example, destroyed all property between Pearl Street and Broadway, from State Street to Maiden Lane. Its origin was traced to a livery stable. Arson was suspected and the finger was pointed to a group of slaves (there being some restless striving for freedom at that time.) Four of the accused blacks were marched up State Street and hanged on Pinkster Hill.

A nucleus of trade was the Market-House which stood in the middle of Broadway near Maiden Lane. There the farmers came to traffic in the daytime; and there, under the shed-like roof, the burghers gathered in the cool of evening to puff their long pipes and talk. A common saying was: "If I had a thousand pounds, I could afford to sit in the market and would not call the Patroon 'uncle.'" Later, public markets sprang up in the center of State Street, on Columbia Street, and at South Pearl and Howard Streets.

Except for farm produce, Albany's commerce came and went largely by ship. Even when the fur-trade was lost and Albany turned to grain and lumber, its riverfront was the most important part of town.

A typical example of the rapid commercial expansion and the opportunities it presented is the case of William James, an Irish immigrant who arrived in the usual penniless condition in 1793. He opened a general store in 1795, a modest place. Two years later he launched a second store on the waterfront to receive produce from farmers. By 1798, he started a tobacco factory. In 1805, he broadened out into a partnership with a New York man, John Flack, and they operated stores in both cities. With his mounting profits, James bought enormous acreages of state lands, and even got some New York City real estate holdings. He loaned money, and he leased and operated salt works in Syracuse (hence the village of Jamesville). He helped promote the Erie Canal and became a bank official. His relatives called him affectionately "The Patroon," and by 1818 he was rich enough to withdraw from business, leaving the management to one of his sons.

William James lived in a big house at State and Green Streets. It was proper for wealthy people to have their mansions in the midst of downtown. There were far more dwellings on Pearl Street and Broadway than there were business houses. The section of Broadway south of State (then known as Court Street) was the most fashionable section.

The first gas lights flickered in 1845. Kerosene lights made their appearance in 1860. And by 1881 electricity began lighting the streets.

Came the railroads, and Broadway bustled with famous hotels—among them the Delavan House and Stanwix Hall. The New York Central and the D. & H. maintained separate depots on Broadway until they combined in Union Station in 1900.

Albany had come of age. There were no more pigs in the streets. But one atrocious eyesore remained—the unkempt waterfront. It was filthy and stinking and thoroughly disreputable. State Street and Maiden Lane ran all the way down to the riverside, where they spawned warehouses, saloons, slaughter-houses, and worse. Moreover, the dull drabness of Victorianism had crept over the city's architecture, crowding out Philip Hooker. Then Marcus T. Reynolds entered the scene. Son of an old, respected Albany family, Reynolds had studied at Williams and Columbia and won a fellowship to study architecture abroad. The medieval buildings, especially those of Gothic style, captivated him.

A century after Hooker had made the city over, Reynolds had a chance to leave his mark. He designed such beautiful buildings as the Pruyn Library (now gone) and the Albany Trust Company (now First American Bank at the corner of State and Broadway). Finally he could abide the waterfront no longer. He drew up a scheme in 1910 for the "creation of a public square by the demolition of dilapidated buildings in the congested area on the river front." He laid it before William F. Barnes, reigning Republican boss of the city. At this point was born one of those rare and fortunate collaborations of two people—the dreamer and the pragmatist—which can produce such astonishing results.

Barnes went Reynolds one better. He happened to know that the D. & H. Railroad was considering a headquarters office building in Albany. He talked the railroad into combining its building plans with the waterfront improvement project. Reynolds, drawing upon the Flemish Gothic style as represented by the town halls of Brussels, Antwerp, Ghent, and Bruges, prepared his plans, believing the use of these prototypes to be appropriate to the city's Walloon and Dutch origins. He wove history into the decoration, with stone beavers and prominent family crests marching across the facade. He also designed a hammered copper replica of the *Half Moon* (measuring six feet and nine inches in length and weighing 780 pounds) to stand atop the central tower 200 feet above the Hudson and point the wind direction.

The D. & H. conveyed to the city the land in front of the grand structure for the Plaza Park. And "Billy" Barnes, seeing what a handsome building it was going to be, undertook to erect the south tower himself as the home of his newspaper, the *Albany Evening Journal.* He even took up personal residence in a fabulous apartment on the top floors of the *Journal* tower.

Marcus T. Reynolds also designed the city's first "skyscraper," the eastern section of the former Home Savings Bank at 11 North Pearl Street. When he proposed to erect a building nine stories tall, the directors were aghast. It would surely topple over! But it stood firm and set the precedent for the burst of skyscraper construction that came in the late '20s.

This time it was the engineers' turn to be skeptical. Albany's underpinnings are notoriously insecure, with deep layers of clay and quicksand to bedrock. There was serious doubt if a 20-story building would stand erect. But the Home Savings Bank went that high in 1927, to be followed skyward by the National Savings Bank, the State Bank, and the enlarged City and County Bank at 100 State Street, now home of Home and City Savings Bank.

The City and County Bank retained Reynolds as its architect, and he added his second most conspicuous touch to the Albany skyline, the fancy French Renaissance tower with its wing-footed Mercury (no longer there). The recesses of the tower were illuminated with colored floodlights until World War II extinguished them.

Adapted from "Pine Palisades Laid Out Zone of Albany Business Area of Today," *Times Union,* December 2, 1951.

★ ★ ★ ★ ★ ★ ★ ★ ★ ★ ★ ★

North Albany

THE ODD SITUATION of the Dutch West India Company sitting in the middle of a Patroon's grant was bound to create friction. For many years the settlement was torn by two questions: to whom did the land beneath Fort Orange belong, and whose authority was to prevail over the outpost? The existence of North Albany as a community set apart may be traced indirectly to that controversy.

The first member of the Van Rensselaer family to set foot on the Patroon's possessions in America was Jan Baptiste, son of the original Kiliaen (deceased), who came as director in 1651 when the quarrel was at the boiling point. Peter Stuyvesant, the West India Company's director-general at New Amsterdam (New York), had ordered that all buildings of the Patroon's people remain at least 600 paces from Fort Orange, and he demarcated the boundary with a circle of posts. In 1652, to emphasize the point, Stuyvesant named the place Beverwyck.

The restriction did not apply to the Patroons, for when Jeremias Van Rensselaer arrived in 1658 to succeed his brother as director of the colony, he took over the same house, which was about 150 feet west of Fort Orange. He resided there until 1666, when the river rose to an unusually high flood stage and swept that house away. By this time the English had seized Beverwyck and renamed it Albany. Jeremias looked farther afield for his new home. He chose a site two miles to the north on a fertile expanse of flatland, watered by a scenic tributary which tumbled down over cascades from the back country.

Jeremias built a gabled, three chimneyed brick homestead, with shutters and loopholes for defense against Indians, and thereby established the site of the later Van Rensselaer Manor House. After the British takeover, the Patroon's domain of Rensselaerswyck was translated into a Manor, in the English sense. Around the Manor House, a self-contained community of Van Rensselaer servants and workers grew into what came to be known as "The Colonie." The magnificent Manor House was erected on a nearby site in 1765, when the old one was doomed by plans to straighten the road to Troy.

Whatever its faults, as a replay of European feudalism, the patroonship gave Albany its golden era. The gleaming carriages that rolled up the avenue through the high iron gates of the Manor House carried nearly every important personage of the Colonies and most of the titled travelers from abroad. The Van Rensselaers knew how to live grandly and had the wealth with which to do so. The grounds, ample and well-groomed, were studded with trees and shrubbery. In their northern reaches rippled a private lake, variously spoken of in later days as the "Scottish Pond" or the "Curling Pond," because of its popularity in winter for the sport imported with newly arrived workers from Scotland. The Patroon's Creek, a stream of good size, sought the Hudson across the Manor House yard, and huge weeping-willow trees drooped along its banks. A bridge crossed the creek at Broadway. It was called the "Kissing Bridge," as a popular courting place for downtown swains and North Albany girls. Each May the family raised a beautiful Maypole in the front yard for all to see.

Stephen Van Rensselaer III, the last to inherit the manorial title under law, married a daughter of Philip Schuyler. Progressive minded, he encouraged the very things that brought about the decay of the Van Rensselaer glories—the American Revolution, the Erie Canal, the railroads. In fact, Stephen turned the first spade of earth for the Mohawk and Hudson Railroad, little dreaming that it would soon (in 1844) despoil his beloved Tivoli Valley.

His son, the last Stephen, remodeled the Manor House in 1840, adding the east and west wings and a stone portico. When Stephen IV died in 1866, his widow, usually referred to as "The Madame," presided over the Manor House alone. She was the kind of grand lady who could say casually, "I think I might run over to Paris tomorrow"—and go.

The coming of the canal across their home acres signified for the aristocratic Van Rensselaers the beginning of the end of their richly genteel way of life. A modern, robust America was emerging, with scant sympathy for either social niceties or the landlord system by which the "Young Patroon" was trying to collect back rents from 900 farms.

Not long after the canal had intruded on the scene, trains of the Mohawk and Hudson began setting fire to the grass along the pleasant banks of Patroon's Creek as they found their low-level outlet through Tivoli Hollow.

The sumptuous Manor House—long acclaimed as the handsomest

dwelling in all the Colonies—found itself caught between the canal and the railroad. Long before the Manor House was abandoned, the surroundings had ceased to be what a Van Rensselaer would call desirable. Commercialism, crass and noisy and dirty, was closing in from all sides. The aging edifice stood rather sadly, though still haughtily, amid the shambles. After the widow of the "last patroon" died in 1875, the house was vacant save for caretakers. Superstition had it that the place was haunted. Mrs. Charles S. Hamlin (the former Huybertie Pruyn) recollected visits there as a girl, when a white spitz dog would growl and bark at the foot of the stairs and refuse to go up. "He sees the ladies this morning," Jane MacLeod, wife of the gatehouse keeper, would say.

In the forlorn last days of the Mansion, people remembered it as being shut off from Broadway by a green picket fence, beyond which grew "the most gorgeous lilacs you ever saw." A Van Rensselaer heir was about to permit its destruction—its stone to go to a lumber warehouse—when Marcus T. Reynolds, the eminent Albany architect, arranged for Sigma Phi fraternity to purchase it for reconstruction on the Williams College campus at Williamstown, Massachusetts. In one of its lapses in historical sensitivity and architectural awareness, Albany allowed the mansion to be taken away.

But that was not the end of the story. During the 1960s, when Greek-letter fraternities were dying out, Sigma Phi gave its chapter house and grounds to Williams College. Again the old house stood idle for almost a decade. Then the college chose its site for a new library wing and was about to demolish the building. Hearing of its impending fate, a Delmar dermatologist, Dr. D. Joseph Demis, came to the rescue. The college was glad to have him cart it away, stone by stone. It was trucked back over the Taconics, and is now hidden away in a secret place in hope of ultimate reconstruction.

The last building extant in North Albany that was a part of the Manor establishment is a narrow brick building at 1144 Broadway. Nowadays its east end faces the street with a sign reading "Sweet Lorraine's Cafe"; for many years it was the "City Line Tavern." This was the Upper Office (or factor's office) where the records of tenant-farmer leases and their rental payments were kept. The Lower Office, to which tenants drove to pay their yearly rents, vanished long since.

Possibly the oldest structure in Albany, the Upper Office was for decades the club-house of the Phoenix Club, a card-playing social circle of prominent North Albany men. In some previous year, a large vault opening from one of its walls had been looked into when it was removed.

Stephen Van Rensselaer, III, contributed significantly to Albany's growth.

It yielded a hoard of old deeds and leases to farms of the Manor, some written on parchment. Club members were using them to start fires in the stove on cold days, when Michael Conners, an insurance man, recognized what they were and salvaged the remainder. Michael was the father of the present Assemblyman, Richard J. Conners.

The last remaining piece of Van Rensselaer land, of the vast holding that was measured, not in acres, but in square miles, laid atop the great North Albany sand and gravel beds. Deposited in glacial time by a stream spilling its load from the northwest, these banks furnished much of the material that has gone into Albany buildings. For many years, the Van Rensselaer Bank, as the beds were known, was visited by wagons whose owners paid the Manor by the load. Initially, the bank extended nearly to Broadway. Only three or four generations ago, North Pearl Street (formerly Orchard Street) was cut through the deposit.

The Van Rensselaer heirs themselves finally sealed the doom of their lifestyle by encouraging North Albany's gargantuan Lumber District. It may have crept upon them unawares. New York State had originally been a paradise of virgin timber. In colonial days, Adirondack lumbermen used spring floods to raft lumber down the river to Albany for loading. When the Erie Canal was built, the western New York forests were within reach, and the lumber business boomed afresh. Lumberjacks felled the white-pine forests and sent the timber on canal barges to North Albany. For decades, Albany reigned as the white-pine distribution center of the world. After the Civil War, lumber from the Great Lakes region began to arrive.

The crucial strip of land was a man-made peninsula lying between the canal and the river—Van Rensselaer property. Across this, lumber was transferred from canal barges to river craft. On the canal side, barges nosed for unloading into more than 40 slips. The lumber was then sorted, graded, and piled for reloading into ships destined for ports of the Atlantic seaboard and beyond.

The Lumber District, by its heydey in the 1870s, had spawned around 50 lumber companies, employed 1,500 men, and handled up to 700,000,000 board feet a year. The Van Rensselaer strip was a veritable city of lumber piles, extending a mile and a quarter northward from Lawrence Street and the Canal Basin. A horse-car line threaded its way among the piles to their northern limit. Offices amidst the slips vied for grandeur, and some were ferried across the river to become residences in the north of Rensselaer when the boom had ended. It was the era of the Lumber Barons—the Sages, Rathbuns, Arnolds, Benedicts, Kibbes, Hubbells, Voses, Weavers, Daltons, Whites, and Thomsons

Stacks of lumber dwarf even hefty Northenders, who handled it as a way of life.

and the rest. Some built their mahoganied mansions along Ten Broeck Street; the Sages reigned philanthropically over Menands, while others converted the hamlet of Ireland's Corners into Loudonville.

Men who worked for these magnates were largely the offspring of those who had fled the potato famine in Ireland—a strong and lusty breed who dressed in red flannel shirts and leather aprons. The area around the Lumber District was so Irish that it became known as Limerick.

A story survives of the Limerick lady, who while riding one day on the horse-car down Broadway, overheard two women discussing North Albany in disparaging terms. As she was leaving the car, she turned to the gossips with a tilt of the chin and said: "Let yez both move to hell. Ye'll find no Irish there."

The lumber-handlers had to be husky. The wood was heavy, the hours were long, and the pressure to work fast was intense. Many were piece-workers, and legends grew of their fabulous feats of strength and of friendly rivalries between the "Limerick Lads" and the "Lock Lads" (the latter being those who dwelt east of Broadway, where Lock 2 of the canal was operated).

When the canal froze up, North Enders took to racing horses along the ice—and of course to skating. But no boats moved. So the lumber-handlers turned ice-handlers. Several large ice-houses (such as the Knickerbocker Ice Company on Knickerbocker Island) hired them to cut ice in the Hudson. One of Limerick's leading families operated a big ice-house, J. Mullen's Sons.

Various professions and businesses related to the canal and the lumber trade naturally flourished in North Albany. The canal boat captains were a fraternity unto themselves. Then there were the drivers, who guided the horses and mules that towed the barges along the canal. The drivers, in turn, relied on folk like the Flinns, who stabled, fed, and tended the animals. Many future Albany business leaders got their start as "tally boys" in the Lumber District, taking their turns swimming the canal with buckets on a plank to bring back beer. Two or three saloons were enterprising enough to send "bumboats" through the slips with ale on tap.

The work was hard for all concerned. At the end of the canal season, a worn-out mare or horse might sell for 50 cents. And, while in one sense the lordly Van Rensselaers may have deplored the trespass, they didn't object to the profit that came from leasing a mile and a half of their waterfront to the lumber interests.

When the railroads could offer cheaper, faster transport, the death knell sounded for the Lumber District. Almost all signs of the District are gone, but Erie Boulevard (which is far short of a boulevard!) traces the old route of the canal.

Adapted from "Old Albany: Lumber Brought Wealth; Patroons Gave Town Golden Age," *Times Union,* November 11, 1951.

The South End

THE SOUTH END WAS the historic birthplace of Albany. It cradled the nucleus of the settlement during the first half-century when brash, earthy little Fort Orange was nosing its way into the edge of the forest. But the recurrent floods drove settlers to seek higher land.

In aftertime, it was here that the Industrial Revolution finally smote Albany with full impact. It was here that the early drama of labor unionism unfolded. It was here that Albany's melting-pot simmered.

But in the beginning things were very simple. An early spectator described life in the South End like this: "They dig a square pit in the ground, cellar-fashion, six or seven feet deep, and as long and as wide as they think proper. They case the earth inside with wood all around the wall, and line the wood with the bark of trees or something else to prevent the caving in of the earth. They floor this cellar with plank, and clapboard it overhead for a ceiling, run a roof of spars clear up and cover the spars with bark and green sods, so that they can live dry and warm in these houses with their families for two, three, and four years."

Every spring the river would rampage, threatening and sometimes overwhelming the area. It forced the Dutch dominies to move the church to a safer location. Yet the church maintained a tangible interest in the South End. The very first deed issued by the city under the Dongan Charter (in 1687) granted all the flood-soaked downriver flats to the Reformed Dutch Church (pastor, Dr. Godfredius Dellius) for a consideration of 390 pounds. The deed defined the tract as "beginning near the place where the old Fort stood and extending along Hudson's River till it comes against the most northerly part of the Island, commonly called Martin Gerritsen's Island" [now the Port of Albany]. Thus the South End became the Dutch Church Pasture—or simply The Pasture—to many generations.

The few houses built on it had been carried off by floods, so it was shunned ground, good for one thing only—grazing. Cattle, kept within the stockade by night, would be driven forth to The Pasture in daytime, wearing a path soon known as Cow Lane. Along the route thus trodden by hoofs, George Washington one day strolled with his General of the Northern Department, Philip Schuyler, to keep a dinner date with Jeremiah Van Rensselaer. In consequence, the path became Washington Street. Now paved, it is called South Pearl Street.

The cows didn't have it all to themselves. With Albany almost constantly in arms, The Pasture—and the ridge known as Johnny Robinson's Hill (ultimately Madison Avenue)—were much used for drilling by the British soldiery and local militia. Indeed, Robinson's Hill was the regular camping-ground of the redcoat forces under Abercrombie and Amherst during the French and Indian War.

The South End once came close to being a Yankee whaling center. Some salty mariners of the New England coast, whose shipping had suffered heavily from encounters with the British Navy, banded together in 1783 to found a town in a more protected location. Thirty of them, mostly Quakers, sent scouts to seek a site. The committee came up the Hudson, fancied the untenanted pasture-land to the south of Albany, and made an offer. The Dutch Church turned them down, determined that Albany should not expand beyond the bounds set by Peter Stuyvesant. Besides, they didn't like Yankees. So the New Englanders decided upon Claverack Landing, founded Hudson, and brought whaling to the river.

Public pressure for the Dutch Church to break up The Pasture into lots eventually prevailed. In 1785, the Board of Aldermen addressed a letter to the church declaring "the necessity of laying out the Pasture to the South of the City into House Lotts, thereby to promote the welfare of this city and the weal of the state." Two years later, the Consistory of the church got around to setting before the aldermen a survey, with a plan for such lots. The auction of lots, begun in 1793, proceeded slowly, bringing at first only $15 to $30 a lot.

Robinson's Hill, a tall ridge on the far side of the Ruttenkill ravine, provided the clay for most of the town's early brick buildings and roadbeds. And when the crest of the hill was scraped down to ease the grade, the earth was used as fill for the ferryboat landing—principal access to the city from Greenbush (Rensselaer)—and a new street, South Ferry. Platoons of fine brick houses sprang up on fields where the militia used to drill.

Things went differently up on the hill slopes. South Pearl Street, as the high water line of the river, became another boundary; above it a house could be safe. There, overlooking a fine sweep of the Hudson River, young Philip Schuyler and Catherine Van Rensselaer Schuyler selected the site for their home. No doubt "Sweet Kitty" had considerable influence in the choice: from the stoop she could look across at her parental homestead (now Fort Crailo). When Schuyler returned from a mission to England in 1762, he found "The Pastures" complete, thanks to his wife, to General John Bradstreet and some idle British Army carpenters. It was Albany's first English-style house. It stands today, a Georgian beauty, the gem of Albany's historic mansions. The street that still forms the northern boundary of the property, Catherine Street, honors the first mistress of that house.

The splendid Schuyler house, with its broad acres and fine fruit orchards, its handsome French landscaping and parterres, its stables and slave quarters, was one of the noted homes of the colonies. Here Philip and Catherine Schuyler practiced the arts of gracious living and noblesse oblige, their guest list a roster of patriots. Schuyler's espousal of the Revolutionary cause, despite his aristocratic heritage and wealth, was as significant in the North as was Washington's in Virginia. Thus the mansion became a focal point in the Revolution and in the shaping of the first free government. In its study, Alexander Hamilton worked on an early draft of the U.S. Constitution. It served as headquarters of the Federalist Party afterward.

The Schuyler house was almost lost to history, as so many other historic homes were. After Schuyler's death, it was put up for sale and passed through many hands. In 1846, it was bought at auction, on a foreclosure, by Ezekiel McIntosh, a wealthy merchant. McIntosh died, and his widow, a true romantic, put the house briefly back into history by using the parlor in which Alexander Hamilton and Betsy Schuyler were wed, to marry Millard Fillmore, the former President. The Fillmores moved to Buffalo and sold the house to John Tracy, a wholesale liquor dealer. Lansing Pendleton bought it in 1884 with the avowed purpose of turning it into a beer-garden, a scheme luckily abandoned. In 1886, the house became an orphanage conducted by the Sisters of St. Francis De Sales. In 1911, the Albany Catholic Diocese was considering tearing it down to build a new orphanage on the site. At this point the state intervened to acquire it. Partially restored, it was opened to the public in 1917.

The Schuylers had neighbors, if such they could be called, distant as they were—the Groesbecks and the Hallenbakes. The Groesbeck family had a farm south of Second Avenue (the locality was known as Groesbeckville well into the 19th century). The Hendrick Hallenbakes, on the uptown side of Schuyler, owned 1,800 acres, separated from Schuyler's by the ravine of the Beaverkill (now running in the Arch Street sewer.) It is unlikely there was animosity between the families, but for many years a cannon stood at South Pearl and Arch Streets to mark the property line.

Hallenbake laid out what was to become Grand Street. He envisioned it as the main southern approach to Albany, insisting that it be 60 feet wide. A lone house stood like a sentry post at Hamilton and Grand as late as 1835. Hallenbake is also credited with having mapped South Pearl Street across his land. The Hallenbakes' private, fenced-in cemetery, 60 feet square, was preempted during the cholera epidemic of 1832 to receive the dead, who were hastily buried in common graves nine feet deep. When those bodies, together with sundry departed Hallenbakes, were moved to Albany Rural Cemetery in 1860 for the widening of Hamilton Street, such crowds collected that the police dispersed them.

One of the earlier Executive Mansions belonged to the South End. The Yates mansion, occupying the hill between the Schuyler house and town, was home to Abraham Yates, financier, descendant of an early Dutch clan and mayor of Albany from 1790 to 1796. Then it passed into the hands of the Kanes, a wealthy mercantile family, who leased it to William H. Seward, Governor from 1839 to 1843. In 1856, banker T. W. Olcott purchased it for use by the principal of the Female Academy. It changed hands again and was razed to make way for the Ash Grove Methodist Church, dedicated in 1865. The superb ash trees surrounding the mansion foreshadowed the name Ash Grove Place. The Ash Grove and Trinity Place vicinity was, during the Victorian era, a high-toned residential locality.

The city proper was amply occupied, indeed crowded, in the 19th century. When immigrants began to roll in, long-term residents moved toward the empty spaces, leaving their homes for newcomers. And come they did, in a great human freshet—the Irish, the Germans, the Italians, the Jews, a smattering of Spanish and Syrian, Polish and Armenian. Out of the vigorous, polyglot, boisterous, two-fisted, rowdy, devout, happy, devil-may-care mixture came much of the city's later vitality—and many of its ablest citizens. The South End was also spawning ground for Albany's latter-day political potentates. From it emerged the O'Connell family. Out of it, too, came scientists like Theobald Smith (née Schmidt), who opened a door for modern medicine by proving that insects may carry disease; and entertainers like Mary McNish (née Flannery), who conquered the opera world.

There were Germans enough in Albany in the early 1800s so that Lutheran services were conducted in both German and English, and classes in South End schools were taught in both languages. A surge of Germans came after 1840, and a second wave when Bismarck was clamping Germany in his iron Prussian vise. Rebels against despotism and military conscription, they populated the erstwhile cow-pasture and worked for a better life.

Oddly, the immigrant Germans—in a town that was historically Holland Dutch—were called "Dutchmen." It was common for them to be hailed along South Pearl Street as "Dutchie," and upper Alexander Street was known as Dutch Hollow for its German, not Dutch, residents.

Jollity and conviviality meant much to these new Albanians. Their favorite social centers—for song-fests, dances, and parties—were Eintrach (or Wink's) Hall, on South Pearl Street, and Cecilia Hall (later Angesser's), on Alexander Street. They also introduced lager beer to Albany.

Among the hardworking German folk were Philip and Theresa Schmidt. They built a home at 54 Alexander Street, and in 1859 a son, Theobald, was born. During vacations from Cornell, where he was earning his way by playing the chapel organ, Theobald was forever fussing with guinea pigs in the backyard; the neighbors thought he was a little "queer." He was certainly extraordinary. Today he is internationally regarded as one of the most significant researchers in the history of medical science. By proving that Texas fever in cattle was carried by ticks, he paved the way for control of yellow fever and malaria, and thereby made the Panama Canal possible.

The Irish influx just about kept pace with the German. Laborers poured in to work on the Erie Canal and stayed to build the early railroads. Those jobs were finished, they fell idle. Their impoverishment was compounded by the Panic of 1837. Demoralized and shunned, they huddled together in the growing South End, pleading for land and talking of organizing. Enterprising business investors could not ignore such a labor market. Before very long, factories sprang up to absorb them.

If there was one sector of the South End that was more militantly Irish than any other, it was the "Connaught Block," the riverfront end of Madison Avenue. Lurid tales spread of what would happen to an outsider trespassing in the "Connaught Block," with its "potato-butchers" (vegetable dealers) and its abundant saloons. The neighborhood boasted of its Monahans and Mulcahys and Gormans. Some of its lads gleaned fame and trophies with their four-oared racing shells on the river.

The Germans and Irish alternated their enormous picnics at Blackman's Bush (later Collings Grove and Dobler Park) on upper Second Avenue. Another popular summertime resort of the pleasure-craving South End was Abbey's Tavern, at the south end of Van Rensselaer Island. On Island Creek, the moat surrounding the island, visitors could rent rowboats or board a two-decked steamer.

Albany had few Jewish residents prior to 1830. There were enough by 1837 to found the first synagogue, on Bassett Street, and by 1851 to take over the South Pearl Street Baptist Church for a synagogue. By 1880, the South End was estimated to have 3,000 Jews. That year the rolls showed no more than 25 Italian families. The full force of Italian immigration came at the beginning of the next century and kept up until immigration quotas in 1921 diminished the flow. By that time the lower Madison Avenue district had become almost exclusively Italian, though a small colony of Spaniards had crept in. Albany even acquired an Italian consulate. For 34 years, Germano Baccelli, a scholarly, bearded private banker, served as consul, gaining high esteem in the Italian community.

The old South End was Albany's great pool of manpower. The pig-iron and stove foundries absorbed much of it during the decades when Albany was the stove-making center of the United States. Wherever the pioneers pushed into the expanding West, they sent back orders for stoves, and Albany supplied them. Such families as the Rathbones, the Ransoms, and the Townsends amassed fortunes in that business. The South End pulsed with the northern industrial boom after the Civil War, and also writhed with its social and economic ills. The iron-moulders, generally well paid as they were, resented such things as inhumanly long hours (many started work at 4 a.m.) and low-wage competition. They especially hated the Berkshire System by which iron-moulders were compelled to have a certain number of boys as helpers.

Iron Moulders Union No. 8, founded in 1859, promptly struck against the Berkshire System. Rioting ensued; stones and brickbats flew. The companies agreed to abolish the system but reinstated it a bit later. More riots followed. The Knights of Labor (predecessor to the A. F. L.) sent in organizers. Even the bellicose Molly Maguires showed up. The industry was shaken. Although the discovery of the Lake Superior iron deposits doomed the Albany stove industry, its end was hastened, no doubt, by the labor troubles. The financial panic of the 1890s delivered the coup de grace.

The Schuyler family returned to prominence on the South End stage in the later 1800s. Captain Samuel Schuyler, a kinsman of the Philip Schuylers, quit school in 1824 to ship as cabinboy on a Hudson River sloop and became a seasoned river man. The growing barge traffic, result of the Erie Canal, gave him an idea. He and his brother, Thomas, founded the Schuyler Towing Line, which reputedly became the largest towing service in the country. Its tugs would haul "tows" up to 80 barges long. The Schuyler brothers built a fortune—then lost it with a night-boat line, but not before Samuel erected another "Schuyler Mansion." This one was a home on Ash Grove Place, with a glass-encircled "crow's nest" in the roof whence he could keep his telescope trained on river traffic.

While Madison Avenue was still Lydius Street, the jumping off point of civilization (a policeman was attacked by a mink there in 1855), the Cathedral of the Immaculate Conception arose on the spine of Robinson's Hill. Bishop John McClosky, first bishop of the young Albany Diocese, went boldly ahead with the $180,000 project. Its future grandeur was manifest, as it rose from a barren hill. The new cathedral was separated from the main town and approachable only by footpaths when it was dedicated in 1852, as yet without steeples.

As industries faded, the star of mercantilism soared higher. South Pearl Street became a business section unto itself. In the '90s and after, it was especially the farmers' shopping district, with shoppers "parking" their teams and wagons in "Farmers' Yard."

Rich and boundless is the lore of the South End. No section of Albany seems to have produced so many amusing anecdotes, curious names, and picturesque characters.

Who hasn't heard of "I, George Krank," who, running for reelection as alderman, coined an immortal campaign slogan? In his previous term, he had the first water line extended along uptilting Second Avenue. In his appeal to the voters, he reminded them: "I, George Krank, I made the water run up Second Avenue!"

Then there was "Poppy" Sawyer. Born a poor boy, he learned the cobbler's trade at an early age. At the outbreak of the Civil War, he shrewdly secured a large supply of boots and shoes and then sold them at inflated war prices. Investing the profits in real estate, he became very wealthy but remained an eccentric throughout his long life on Herkimer Street. He adhered to Civil War style in apparel, with drab high-buttoned coat, tall boots, high collar, and stovepipe hat. His secondhand garments were always rumpled, yet he maintained a stiff dignity as he strode the streets, ignoring apples and tomatoes thrown at his silk hat by urchins. He rode in every parade, and was reputed to go around making repairs on his widespread real estate holdings with his own hands.

Devoutly religious, "Poppy" gave away most of his money. He loved to build churches. Hope Baptist Church, a Baptist Chapel on Madison Avenue, and a chapel at Kenwood were among his benefactions. He is also remembered as the principal founder of Memorial Hospital.

Adapted from "The South End Was Albany's Real Cradle: Revolutionary Capital of North, It Was Birthplace of Industry," *Times Union,* September 2, 1951.

★ ★ ★ ★ ★ ★ ★ ★ ★ ★ ★ ★ ★ ★

Capitol Hill

THE HILLCREST STARTED leveling off 200 feet above tidewater of the Hudson, and the slant was steep. Even Fort Frederick (later Fort Albany) did not presume to stand at the top of the hill—only two-thirds of the way. The early Dutch burghers ventured up its slopes to pluck blueberries or fragrant azaleas, to hunt quail, to bury their dead, or to hang their malefactors. It was a rather forbidding place where rattlesnakes abounded and a fierce Indian or two might suddenly appear.

Yet this untamed hilltop was destined to be Albany's acropolis. When the Legislature finally decided it was time for the State of New York to have a real Capitol, this was the site it settled upon. (Humankind, since the time of ancient Greece and Rome, has fancied hilltops for grand structures.) The hill, to be sure, did not figure in the selection of Albany as the capital city; that was almost accidental. After "meeting around" in different cities of the Hudson Valley, the Legislature began to find transferring the heap of needed documents onerous. The body happened to be meeting in Albany in 1797 when it voted to erect a "public building" for records.

That building, State Hall (at State and Lodge), was by no means a Capitol. The lawmakers still met at the Stadt Huys. Nor was any act passed making Albany the capital city. But the construction of the building did indicate that the Legislature was putting down roots.

After the Revolution, when Fort Albany was eradicated from the middle of the State Street incline and its stone blocks were dispersed around town, people grew more interested in the summit. To celebrate New York's ratifying of the U. S. Constitution in 1788, a "Federal Bower" was hastily raised at the top—a wooden framework 154 feet long, supported by four pillars and wreathed with flowers and greenery. Beneath the bower, tables were spread for public feasting, and 13 toastswere drunk to the newly established states of the Union.

Then, for a period, the future locus of the Capitol became Pinkster Hill, so known for its use by the black slaves and freedmen of the city for their yearly Pinkster Festival. Though these fetes were occasions for merriment, the tradition was of religious origin. They were held at the time of Pentecost, or Whitsuntide (the seventh week after Easter). The word Pinxter was a Dutch corruption of Pentecost. As the festival occurred while the azaleas, or june pinks, were abloom on the hill, it was easy to corrupt "Pinxter" a shade more, to "Pinkster" for the flower.

An oblong space was laid out, bordered by booths which sold refreshments and ran games of chance. Madcap revelry held sway, with the beat of tom-toms and African dancing. White citizens (some of them owners of slaves) flocked to watch the sport and patronize the booths. Indians were occasional sideline spectators. The Pinksterfest took on some aspects of a circus, with wild-animal exhibits and tightrope acrobatics. The perennial master of the revels was "King Charley," an ancient but agile black man in motley.

After some seasons the affair got rowdy. A city ordinance of 1811 prohibited the further erection of booths for the sale of "liquors, mead, sweetmeats" and the like. The last Pinkster Parade took place in 1822, and "King Charley" died in 1824, reputedly aged 125. (Slavery was abolished in New York State in 1827.)

A darker side of the hill is revealed in its other name, Gallows Hill. It was not unusual in the 18th century, when robbery, arson, and murder were capital crimes, to see white-garbed prisoners being led up the steep Jonckers Street grade to their doom. Actually, the scaffold was a little off to the south, on the margin of the Ruttenkill ravine (later to be filled and covered by Hudson Avenue). Crowds gathered to witness the hangings as if they were a form of entertainment. As late as 1794, four black slaves were hanged on the hill, convicted of setting fire to Leonard Gansevoort's stable, a fire which spread calamitously, destroying 26 buildings in the heart of town. Someone had to be punished, and slaves were often blamed for fires.

At the north edge of the hill, between present-day Eagle and Hawk Streets, were graveyards. Beyond them was a smaller ravine, a branch of the Sheridan Avenue valley, with a similarly grim past. It was there that the patriot militia took Tories and spies for summary execution by firing squad during the Revolution.

Such ghastly doings had no bearing on the selection of the hill for the State Capitol, but the Pinksterfests did, in an indirect way. Those primitive carnivals helped to develop a well-trodden open rectangle that came to be known as the Public Square, much used for recreational and festive activities, as well as military drill. Meanwhile, Philip Hooker, in his guise as city superintendent of streets, had been busily reducing the strenuous grade of the State Street hill, as fast as manual labor, teams, and wagons could have an effect.

When in 1804 it became known that the Legislature was in a mood to build a "state house" in Albany, the city itself tipped the scales by donating an ample portion of the Public Square for the site and shouldering part of the cost. In return, the city was to use some of the space for municipal offices and meeting rooms. The state accepted, and engaged Philip Hooker to design the first Capitol.

The detailed, quasi-official account of Albany's two Capitol buildings has been told (by this writer) in the book, *Capitol Story*. Suffice it to say here that the cornerstone was laid in 1806 by Mayor Philip Schuyler Van Rensselaer, and that the stone of that first building is set into a fourth-level wall of today's Great Western ("Million Dollar") Staircase. The comparatively small first Capitol faced squarely down the wide thoroughfare of State Street. It sported a Grecian type portico of four Ionic pillars and a cupola surrounded by minor pillars. The bell of the historic Stadt Huys was hung in this cupola. This old Capitol served the state with increasing inadequacy for 70 years until it was demolished in 1883, with the new Capitol rising behind it.

At the time the first Capitol was built, only three dwellings shared the location, with here and there a "group of reclining cows." It happened that the spanking new structure was officially opened in the 200th anniversary year of Henry Hudson's voyage. The event marked a dramatic turning point in the career of the city. Now it was in reality the capital of New York State, and the building which attested the fact was by far the most impressive structure in the unattractive old Dutch town. Albany began liking itself better, taking more pride in how it looked to strangers. The hill with the rather unsavory background henceforth began to gather prestige and to become a desirable place of residence. People of wealth and social status commenced to build homes on "little" State Street to the south of the new Capitol. This in turn inspired the burgeoning of educational institutions in the vicinity.

In January 1813, some prominent citizens met at the Capitol to discuss establishing an Albany Academy. They had before them the city's offer to donate a good site along the Public Square, together with an estimated $12,000 to be realized from the sale of the lot and materials of the old jail-house. Some $30,000 would remain to be raised by subscription. The meeting acted favorably. The Boys' Academy, as it was commonly known, was to be partly a military school (the War of 1812 was in progress). It was to be located north of the Capitol, across Washington Avenue (still called Lion Street at the time).

An obstruction, a rather large clay hillock strewn with rubbish, had to be removed before the Academy could be built. A goodly amount was moved to fill in the ravine where Tory prisoners had been shot, and Elk Street was laid over it.

Philip Hooker was chosen as the architect for the Albany Academy, and he endowed it with a style "the most chaste in the city." This time he omitted Grecian columns, but designed a masterpiece of a cupola topped by weathervanes. It was Hooker's "American classicism" in full stride. The Academy was completed in 1816 and opened with almost as much fanfare as the Capitol. Its "campus," enclosed by a neat iron picket fence, was designated Academy Park. Not a public school, it evolved into a school for boys of "the best families." Among its early students who achieved renown were Joseph Henry and Herman Melville.

Joseph Henry was hardly from a "best family"—a penniless rural lad who had come into Albany seeking employment. Lacking money for tuition, he nevertheless walked boldly up to the Academy when it opened and presented himself as a would-be student, having decided to be a natural scientist. His intelligence and aptitude were such that he was accepted for night classes and special tutoring. In a few months he had learned enough to teach in a nearby country school to finance his further Academy studies. Afterward he became a faculty member and ran experiments with electricity in an upper classroom. By 1829, he was able to report his discovery of electromagnetic induction—the basic principle of the telegraph and the electric motor. By connecting wires, he rang a bell in a distant room. Samuel F. B. Morse made a fortune with Henry's discovery, while Henry was content with his appointment as the first director of the Smithsonian Institution.

Herman and Gansevoort Melville, who entered the Academy in 1830, also had difficulty with the tuition. The Melvilles were far from rich in 1830, but their grandfather, General Peter Gansevoort, was one of the school's founders and a trustee. The Melvilles had just moved to Albany from New York, where Allan Melville (husband to Maria Gansevoort) had been successful for a time as an importer but then went bankrupt. The Gansevoort family supplied funds to give Allan a fresh start in Albany and pay the tuition for the boys at the Academy. Herman, only 11 years old, studied "ciphering books" (mathematics)

The spectacular 1911 Capitol fire fed on irreplaceable documents in the State Library.

with Joseph Henry. In his second year he was awarded a "premium" for being "first best" in class, an honor which the *Albany Argus* reported. Fate dealt the Melville family a second blow in January, 1832, when Allan fell ill and died of a fever. Herman and his brother, Gansevoort, were withdrawn from school to go to work.

At that period ordinary folk in Albany complained that the Academy "gave an education to one or two hundred young men of rich families, while the great body of the 6,000 youth of humble rank were neglected." A year after the Academy opened, the building for a radically different type of boys' school was finished not far away. This was the Lancaster School, on the west side of Eagle Street, cornering with Tiger Street (soon to be Lancaster Street). The pattern for this school, originated in England by Joseph Lancaster, was devised to widen instruction for more pupils by utilizing uppergrade students to help teach the younger. While this school lasted, some 10,000 boys were given education they may not otherwise have had. Public, tax-supported education got started during the 1830s, and the Lancaster School closed its doors in 1836. Its building was leased in 1838 for the newly founded Albany Medical College.

In 1863 the Albany Academy celebrated its semi-centennial; Herman Melville, by then an author of some renown, served as a member of the alumni committee. He attended the event, accepting a seat on the platform for the ceremonies.

Today the Albany Academy building is designated the Joseph Henry Memorial and is the solitary building of Philip Hooker's design still standing in its entirety. In front stands a fine statue of the great inventor, unveiled in 1928. When the Academy, as a school, moved to Academy Road in 1931 (a new street opened as its approach), the city purchased the original school building for its Board of Education, and it serves today as the administrative headquarters for the city schools.

During 1824-5, the Marquis de Lafayette, French hero of the American Revolution, paid a farewell visit to the nation he helped liberate. The warm reception he received everywhere turned the visit into a triumphal tour. He appeared in Albany four times, the first in September, 1824. The following year he paused here twice in passing through to and from the west, going on to Boston. He arrived the fourth time, coming from Vermont, accompanied by that state's governor. As a climax to his tour, he was feted at the Capitol and toasted by Daniel Webster, among others. The Legislature commissioned a portrait of Lafayette which was painted by Charles Ingham, and until recent time hung in the Executive Chamber of the Capitol. It was not returned after the Chamber's restoration.

The impact of Lafayette's visits was such that the city changed the name of Sand Street, west from Academy Park, to Lafayette Street. A remote sequel to all this adulation of the French hero cropped up a century later when Alfred E. Smith was Governor.

In 1924 a three-man committee, headed by Mayor William S. Hackett, was named to study the matter of a state office building to bring together various departments and agencies which were scattered all over town paying high rents. One site considered was the built-up area between Academy Park and the State Education Building. That thought was discarded because a high-rise structure would "blanket" the Education Building from the east and overshadow the Capitol itself. The committee, in its 1925 report, did recommend that the state acquire roughly half of that area in from Washington Avenue "and convert the same into a park, thus preventing for all time the erection thereon of objectionable structures and permanently enhancing the setting of the Capitol."

Around this time some realty agents were quietly buying up options on business properties then lining Washington Avenue across from the Capitol. One such person visited Joseph Fiaccabrino, a young Italian barber who held a five-year lease on his Capitol Barber Shop and Beauty Parlor. The agent asked Joe how much he figured his furnishings and lease were worth, if the building he rented from were sold. Joe had a nice trade going and no desire to move. He said $8,000. The agent thrust $500 on him as a down payment, just in case.

Worried, Fiaccabrino inquired around and was told that Joseph P. Kennedy, the Boston financier who sired famous sons, was planning to erect a multi-story office building between the Capitol and the Academy. By Joe's telling, when Governor Al Smith heard of this he hit the ceiling and had the state purchase the whole area and clear it for a park. Stymied on the hill, Joe says, Kennedy turned downtown and got the ten-storied Standard Building (112 State Street) put up instead. This may very well be, though positive proof is lacking.

It turned out that Governor Smith—one of Fiaccabrino's regular customers—actually had plans for a Capitol State Park, to embrace the Albany Academy and its grounds as well as the adjacent area to Hawk Street. He intended to achieve this with funds from a huge bond issue for state parks recently approved by the voters. Joe, the barber, swears that Al Smith even hoped to build a new Executive Mansion alongside the Academy, facing Eagle Street.

A Commission for a State Office Building was set up and it recommended a 32-story structure on the present Swan Street site of the

Governor Alfred E. Smith State Office Building. Smith signed a bill appropriating $2,600,000 for that purpose in January, 1927. Concurrently the Legislature authorized the Commission to purchase "for the purpose of a state park" all properties lying between Washington Avenue, Elk Street, North Hawk Street, and Academy Park. The lawmakers had nixed Smith's grand scheme for a Capitol State Park by slashing a million from his Executive Budget, including $300,000 for purchase of the Academy building—but they had given him the Lafayette State Park.

Meanwhile, the Standard Building downtown went into construction simultaneously with the State Office Building. A search of title deeds reveals the builder as the Standard Construction Company, manifestly a front for the Socony-Vacuum Oil Company, which took over the building after it was completed and stuck the big night-lighted "Flying Red Horse" on the roof. Vague hints suggest that Joseph P. Kennedy had a hand in floating the venture. He was a heavy investor in Standard Oil stock. At any rate, Kennedy became the outright owner of the Standard Building, through a roundabout purchase transaction in 1950. It was sold by his widow, Rose Kennedy, a few years after his death in 1969, and is now the Albany County Office Building.

And what of Joe Fiaccabrino, the barber? He was ousted from his beloved shop, not by Joe Kennedy, but by the State of New York. Luckily he found a niche for a new shop on the State Street side of Capitol Park, and went on trimming the tresses of political bigwigs. With the years, he gravitated into managing the DeWitt Clinton Hotel barber-shop. At the present writing, he was still plying his trade at a one-man shop in the Wellington Hotel, where Mario M. Cuomo came for a well-publicized special haircut soon after he became Governor.

But that all occurred later. In 1829, feeling squeezed, the Legislature voted to pay the city $17,500 for its share in the Capitol. The city applied the money to erecting a City Hall on Eagle Street, diagonally across from the Capitol. Once again, Philip Hooker had a major architectural job to do. That City Hall, topped by a dome, burned in midwinter 1880. A Boston architect, H. H. Richardson, was at that time engaged in designing the Senate side of the new Capitol. He was retained to apply his rich talents to the present City Hall.

The next important addition to Capitol Hill was the State Hall, now the Court of Appeals. Constructed with marble quarried by convicts of the state penitentiary at Sing Sing, this edifice was also nobly domed and pillared. Its initial purpose was to relieve overcrowding in the Capitol and to allow for the storage of state records. In 1917, when the State Hall was converted into a home for the state's highest court, the magnificent Court of Appeals Chamber, one of H. H. Richardson's great rooms, was moved intact—walls, ceiling, fireplace, and all—from the third floor of the Capitol.

Catastrophe struck Capitol Hill in the small hours of March 29, 1911, when fire broke out in the west portion of the Capitol. Before the flames were controlled, they had virtually wiped out the State Library, which occupied the upper floors of that wing. The bitter irony of that tragedy was that if the contractors had met their deadline, the Library would have been safely installed in the State Education Building. That many-pillared structure was formally dedicated in October, 1912, and the State Library was resurrected in the splendid quarters designed for it by Henry Hornbostel.

In the late '20s, another occurrence on Capitol Hill mesmerized the city. The Fort Frederick Apartments building was jacked up, set on rollers, and slowly trundled from Swan and Washington to the south corner of Swan and State Streets. The tenants all the while remained in their homes. The tricky operation made way for the State Office Building previously discussed. During its construction, the area between the Capitol and its site was cleared of crowded buildings, commercial and residential, to allow for an open esplanade. With this edifice, the modern architectural note was first struck on Capitol Hill. At its pinnacle of 388 feet, 7 inches, it gave the Hill at last the observation tower it had failed to get on the crest of the Capitol.

Fire delivered a second tragic blow in the near vicinity of the Capitol on May 19, 1940, with the destruction of the exquisite Harmanus Bleecker Hall. "The Hall," by far Albany's most plush theater for half a century, had been constructed using a bequest by Harmanus Bleecker, a leading citizen of old Dutch stock. The luxurious auditorium had a ceremonial opening on October 9, 1889. On its proscenium curtain was painted a huge and excellent rendering of Henry Hudson's *Half Moon* at anchor in the river. Its ornate lobby widened into a circular amphitheater whose centerpiece was an impressive marble fountain splashing into a pool where goldfish swam and swam. Numerous famous actors performed here, from Elenora Duse and Anna Held to the entire Barrymore clan.

In its latter days Harmanus Bleecker Hall came under lease by the Fabian chain of theaters and showed movies (usually "class films") in intervals between live stage performances. It was on a movie night that it burned. The fire evidently started in an upper balcony where smoking was permitted. It spread fast and towered high. Like the

Capitol fire, it claimed one life, that of a well-liked ticket-taker, Tex, who lingered too long in the rear of the lobby, watching the flames through the little glass window of a swinging door. The lobby roof, its beams unpinned, caved in on him.

Adapted from "Capitol Hill: Acropolis of Albany," *Times Union,* January 13, 1952.

Washington Park

"A BEAUTIFUL PARK in a city is a great moral power." That concept, set forth by the Albany Institute when it laid before the Common Council a startling proposal for a fine municipal park, was by no means so widely accepted in 1868 as it would become during the ensuing decade. Once the populace realized what it was getting—the 90 acres of gracious space, elegantly landscaped, with its flowerbeds, 1,000 trees, monuments, even a good-sized lake—it went into raptures over Washington Park.

Undoubtedly Albany's park project was partly inspired by the example of New York City's already famous Central Park, which had been under development since 1858 and was not yet completed. The designers of Central Park, Frederick Law Olmsted and Calvert Vaux, in fact submitted a plan for Washington Park, but they were not engaged for the job. Its designers were a local firm of Bogart & Cuyler.

The Institute's dream-park had not yet come to focus on a location, mentioning Arbor Hill or the Sheridan Avenue upper ravine as possibilities. But its idea sparked the city into action. When the Common Council voted the creation of Washington Park on May 5, 1869, the former Washington Square, long used as a military drill and parade ground, was part of the terrain made available.

Albany had always been a rather cramped town, lacking even the amenity of a village green, such as graced New England towns. This antique river port, while spreading slowly beyond its hill-crest, was still living largely cooped behind its Victorian fences and walls, but was subconsciously itching to stretch its legs and breathe deep. Washington Park was the release it had been craving. The park generated the city's first great surge of civic pride since the building of the Capitol.

Another thing. The park had a significant impact on residential development to the westward. Well-to-do and socially elite families hastened to build fine homes around its perimeter. Illustrative of its effect on realty values was the fact that properties on Englewood Place assessed at $9,500 in 1875 had shot up to $175,000 by 1891.

William Cullen Bryant's campaign for Central Park in New York in 1857 established a precedent. Professor David Murray spoke of it in his prophetic paper at the June meeting of the Albany Institute in 1863: "American cities are just waking up to the necessity of providing themselves, before it is too late, with parks. No city government is wise which neglects to provide suitable and ample pleasure grounds for its citizens. . . . The feverish, restless brain is cooled and soothed by the fresh breeeze and the cooling shade. . . . Men are wiser, better, more temperate, more loving, when they have wandered amid trees and by waterfalls and heard birds sing and children laugh and play."

The Institute did not consider it extravagant to estimate 250 acres as a desirable size for such a park to be placed in the Arbor Hill section. Instead, the city allocated land above Willett Street, a considerable portion of which had been the old State Street burial grounds. Many of the graves had been previously transferred to the Albany Rural Cemetery, and the vacated spaces had since become a resort for "vicious idlers."

Here, as in other cities, the resting places of the dead had preserved areas from being engulfed by the cities of the living. Washington Park also drew upon another longstanding tradition. Most cities provided space for public squares where the regimentals could drill. In 1806, a rectangle above Willett Street was designated for such a purpose and called the Middle Public Square. In 1809, it was renamed Washington Square. As part of the pine barrens which had hemmed early Albany in on the west, the Washington Square plot was remote enough from civilization that it made an ideal place for a powder-house.

The danger of explosion of ammunition stores was a constant headache for Albany all through the time it was a military outpost. Every so often the town magazine would blow up and create a panic. The Council adopted in 1786 an ordinance "for the better securing of the city of Albany from the danger of gun powder."

Washington Square was chosen. When Fort Frederick was dismantled, some of its stone, as well as the enormous lock-and-key to its ammunition stores, went into the new powder-house. As the city expanded, the powder-house had to migrate westward again into Westland Hills (hence Magazine Street). The historic old lock and key now repose at the Albany Institute of History and Art.

Schoolgirls, on an outing which obviously required a hat, cluster in Washington Park gazebo.

In 1869, the Common Council passed its ordinance for creation of a park. A board of park commissioners was appointed and ground was broken in 1870. The park grew piecemeal. The park lake was excavated in 1873. The lakehouse and nearby bridge were constructed in 1875. The lake occupied the depression left by a stream which had been a tributary to the Beaverkill. Fountains were built at either end to spout water high in the air.

How Albany loved that lake! It was stocked with several varieties of fish. Swans floated on its surface, as did "swan-boats" which could be hired. A rich aquatic garden, including Egyptian lotus, was developed in shallows along the rim. Lake Avenue was so named. The maples and elms already shading the land were joined by many new specimens, including novelties from the fine botanical collection of Erastus Corning, Jr., at his Glenmont estate.

A deer paddock was provided at the far west end of the park, with enough other animals fenced in to give Albany for many years a modest menagerie. The locale was known as Deer Hill, and a refectory was at hand for cooling drinks and ice cream.

Near Madison Avenue was Overlook Hill. There it was that, for some memorable years in the 1880s, an Ice Palace was erected for winter carnivals. The palace would be stormed by "enemy forces" amid the glare of Roman candles, Greek fire, and bombs. Along with the carnival came skating on the lake and bobsled racing down the Madison Avenue hill. A Tanglefoot Snowshoe Club also used to sponsor snowshoe races in the park.

In the good old summertime, "a turn around the park" was both the pleasure and the fashion, when fancy carriages, high-wheeled bicycles, and lace-fringed parasols were in vogue. People of affluence kept large stables on the fringes of the park and it was usual to see fine horses being exercised around the lake. The croquet grounds were a feature of the park long before the tennis courts.

Washington Park was finished just in time and made to order for the bicycling fad. During the 1890s, thousands of young folk turned out on a warm evening, pedaling their way in a constant procession around and around Washington Park's drives. This practice grew to be a menace to pedestrians. Ultimately the police ordered the bike paraders out of the park and they adjourned to the new macadamized streets of the Pine Hills.

The original lakehouse was somewhat baroque in style. Bands performed in concert from a pagoda-like stand on its roof. Its wide piazza was boarded in as a warming house for skaters in winter. When the undertimbers began rotting dangerously, the beloved old structure was replaced during 1928-9 by the present lakehouse.

For a city to put more than a million dollars into something as non-utilitarian as a public park in those days was something to brag about. Albany especially boasted that the charm of Washington Park was its simplicity, its naturalness—that it did not strive for bizarre effects.

It was not long before sculpture began to appear. The first introduction of art into the park was the memorial bust of Dr. James H. Armsby, a co-founder of the Albany Medical College. The bronze bust, cast in Paris and donated to the park by the Albany sculptor, Erastus Dow Palmer, was unveiled in 1879. Standing on its 14-foot granite column, identified by the sole word, "Armsby," it has perplexed many visitors a century after Armsby's death.

The second gift of sculpture, the Robert Burns statue, came to the park in an unusual way. Lachian McPherson arrived in Albany in 1819 from his native Scotland and became janitor of the Capitol and treasurer of the St. Andrew's Society. A frugal man, he laid away his modest earnings. When he died, his son, John, succeeded him as janitor. Neither John nor his sister, Mary, ever married, and they lived penuriously, squirreling away money. John died first. When his sister passed on, it was discovered that they had accumulated between $30,000 and $40,000, a considerable amount at that time. Mary McPherson left the money in her will for the erecting of a statue to the beloved Scottish poet, Robert Burns, fulfilling a hope which had long been cherished in the hearts of the Scottish citizens of Albany. Charles Calverley, a former Albanian, was chosen as sculptor and the statue was completed in 1888. For its unveiling, letters were sent by John Greenleaf Whittier, Oliver Wendell Holmes, and Andrew Carnegie.

The conspicuous King Memorial fountain, representing Moses smiting the rock, also has its story. Rufus H. King, president of the New York State Bank and a director of the Albany Insurance Company, died in 1867. His son, J. Howard King, attending the Centennial Exposition in Philadelphia in 1876, was deeply impressed with the Bartholdi fountain on display. He wrote the French sculptor (who later created the Statue of Liberty) about purchasing the statue for Albany's park. Bartholdi visited the city, agreed to sell it, but regretted he would not be able to attend to its removal here because he had commitments in Europe. Fearful of moving it without the sculptor's supervision, King dropped the plan.

His brother, Henry L. King, in failing health, returned from a futile quest for a cure in Europe determined to raise a statue in the park in memory of their father. He bequeathed $20,000 for that purpose. Several sculptors submitted models which were publicly displayed in the city. The choice fell to J. Massey Rhind, a young sculptor who had recently come to New York from Scotland. The Moses Monument, modeled loosely after some Michaelangelo renderings, helped establish Rhind's reputation.

Washington Park had been planned as a perfect rectangle, to extend all the way up to Lake Avenue along Western Avenue on the north. A curious circumstance intervened. Through a series of land speculations, some of the lots there had come into possession of William Barnes, father of the future Republican political boss of Albany. Certain other lots on Robin Street belonged to a big-scale real estate operator of those times, Andrew E. Brown. Barnes or Brown, or both, held out for exorbitant prices when the park commissioners tried to buy the properties. The commission finally threw up its hands in disgust and ruled that corner out of the park plans. Consequently, a handful of wealthy people found themselves in a unique position—able to live in manorial splendor with a beautiful city park for a dooryard.

This neighborhood presents the first example in Albany of something akin to zoning. By mutual agreement of all the owners, the property deeds were tightly hedged with restrictions. Some of the lumber barons of North Albany's old Lumber District built fabulous homes there. The widow of William Barnes, a daughter of Thurlow Weed, cut through Thurlow Terrace, naming it for her father, and erecting a mansion which became the home of James Fenimore Cooper, descendant of the novelist. The "Fenimore Cooper House," as everyone called it, was torn down some years ago.

Willett Street, with its fashionable town houses and apartment buildings, became Albany's "Central Park South" (although it lay on the east). It had been named for Colonel Marinus Willett, a hero of the Revolutionary War. The city decided to honor this resident of New York City because, as second in command under Albany's Peter Gansevoort, he distinguished himself at Fort Stanwix.

Adapted from "Washington Park Result of Institute Idea: Albany Group Sired Proposal To Meet City's Spiritual Need," *Times-Union,* June 3, 1951.

West Albany

THE MOHAWK & HUDSON Railroad, in 1844, abandoned its original Pine Hills terminus and laid its rails through the only logical exit out of Albany—the gulch of Patroon's Creek, which someone with classical tastes had christened Tivoli Hollow. That sensible change of route seeded a lusty boom-town—West Albany. Fortunes were made and lost in that fabulous overnight community whose name soon was known from Boston to San Francisco, though it never even achieved the status of an incorporated village. In the suddenness of its appearance upon a hitherto vacant space on the map, West Albany rivaled the oiltowns just then popping up in the forests of Western Pennsylvania. Its later decline, too, was precipitous. But what a heydey it enjoyed.

When the Mohawk & Hudson ran its first train from Albany to Schenectady in 1831, there were no ground rules for railroad civil engineering. Nobody knew what steam could be made to do, and nobody knew how much power it would require to haul freight uphill. At first the idea of a direct route from downtown Albany to Schenectady seemed easy: the surface was reasonably level across the Pine Bush. The difficult part was ascending the hill from the river. If latter day trains sometimes required a "pusher" engine to get up the grade of the West Albany Cut, one can imagine how the early boilers on wheels must have wheezed and grunted past the Tivoli Falls and Tivoli Lake (the latter then a city reservoir). It doesn't seem to have occurred to anyone in the beginning that the Patroon's ravine would be the logical passageway out of downtown Albany to the west, even if it required routing the tracks around a bit to the north. When first the tracks were laid through Tivoli Hollow, the engines didn't so much as blow a whistle for West Albany.

At its upper end, the Patroon's gully broadened out toward the

Schenectady Turnpike, and there the railroad erected a long shed for car storage and a little shanty for a switchman. They named the two buildings Spencerville. Such were the humble beginnings of West Albany. Three families—the Duffys, the Cobees, and the Rileys—farmed in the vicinity. The woods between were so thick that the families hardly knew they had neighbors until they heard the roosters crowing. Owen Duffy divided some of his land into lots and sold them to developers who laid them out along the streets of West Albany. Duffy's widow is said to have been offered $105,000 for the rest of the land. She refused—and died in poverty.

At mid-century the major impetus for growth came when the New York Central Railroad consolidated the several short lines across the state and created an immediate need for repair shops somewhere along the route. Erastus Corning, ex-Mayor of the city and first president of the Central, used his influence to place the shops here. (Appreciative residents named West Albany's Corning Street in his honor. They played it safe by naming Richmond Street for Dean Richmond, second president of the railroad.)

The railroad bought 350 acres at Spencerville, some from farmers, others from the Van Rensselaers who had originally held title to it all. The New York Central then renamed the place West Albany. Shop buildings and a roundhouse were slapped up, miles of switchyards were laid out, and a fine residence was built for the station-agent. The first to occupy the house was Captain Joseph Mather. Mather had earned his title as skipper of a Hudson River sloop and had come to Albany as a young man to seek a career in river navigation. He entered the lucrative towing business and stayed put until the railroad lured him away. He was a civic-minded gent, it appears, who took a serious interest in the area and helped develop West Albany.

Downtown skeptics viewed the deal with a cynical eye, implying that the railroads were getting so rich they had to think up tricks to dodge taxes. Imagine their surprise when twenty acres of pens for cattle, sheep, and hogs were spread out in labyrinthine chains across the adjacent fields. The fences were high, and the pens were paved with cobblestones. (To this day, anyone who scrapes away the top-soil on the meadows where pens stood will find cobbles beneath.) The railroad moguls envisioned West Albany as a livestock center ranking with Buffalo and Chicago.

It was not all that farfetched a dream at the moment. Albany had been meatmarket to the continental armies during the Revolution. The industry which thus got going here continued during the early decades of the 1800s, this being a convenient place for farmers to drive their stock for slaughter or for shipment to slaughterhouses elsewhere. The winning of the Great Plains, however, had so expanded the country that it had left the raising of beefcattle only a localized business in the east. A pessimistic newspaper opined in 1850 that the packing trade had deserted Albany "never to return." That paper was obviously insensitive to the possibilities of the railroads. In fact, Albany's meat production was on the eve of returning in a way never before dreamed.

The New York Central, incorporated as the first trunk line probing into the Midwest, afforded a means of safe, rapid transport for steaks-on-the-hoof. For Albany, the important fact was that, while journeying to their doom, the animals had to be taken off the trains to be fed and watered, or they would lose weight and sicken. Albany was just about a day's journey from the previous feeding stop, Buffalo.

Building on that function, West Albany expanded into a great trading center for the packing industry which was growing phenomenally after the Civil War. By 1875, an average of 103 carloads of livestock passed through West Albany each day. In 1880, a total of 100,000 cattle and 150,000 sheep changed hands at the stockyards, many being destined for shipment to Europe. For a long time the cattle came chiefly out of Ohio, Illinois, Kentucky, and Iowa. When the Texas Longhorns joined the throng, Albany welcomed them.

The main drag of West Albany—Exchange Street—memorializes those rambunctious times. The location was, literally, a stock exchange. And trading brought big money. Transactions were cash-on-the-barrelhead. There were no such things as bank checks; in fact, for a long time there was little "folding green." Traders were wont to carry silver dollars in big leather pouches. When bills came back into fashion, the dealers were said to carry fat green wads stuffed in their boots. Once an unwary sheep trader with a big supply of silver dollars on his person was shot and robbed, his body dumped in the woods nearby. (His murderer was caught, tried, and executed.)

Violence was extreme during the railroad strikes of the 1890s. Labor troubles approached a pitch of civil war when the railroad hired Pinkerton detectives. Meanwhile, cattle died by the hundreds in the cars, stranded on the tracks because no one would unload them. The stench which wafted into West Albany must have been terrific. Another time many animals perished was during the Blizzard of '88. With the trains stalled outside West Albany, rescue efforts failed, and many head of cattle froze to death in the cars.

The West Albany cattle yards also spawned a horse-market. Herdsmen required quick, agile horses to control the cattle in the yards. Soon carloads of horses were arriving from the plains for that purpose. In time, spirited western ponies were brought in "wild" and broken at West Albany yards for sale to easterners desiring horses for recreation or transportation purposes. The usual first step in breaking the "green" horses was to tie sandbags across their backs and let them bounce around for a while. It became commonplace to see a span of magnificent Montana ponies being driven through the streets of Albany.

West Albany urchins had the thrills of the Wild West at their very doorsteps and could get paying jobs helping break horses or hiring out to private shippers who wanted their cattle through the gates first. The work was exciting: the boys would sit astride frisky ponies and prod the bellowing cattle with eight-foot poles.

Naturally, with drovers and speculators over-running the place, hotels sprang up in the area. Three astute investors—Andrew Hunter, Nathaniel Gallup, and D. D. T. Moore—bought tracts bordering the New York Central domain, built hotels, and laid out feeding-yards for cattle. The best-known caravansary in West Albany proper was the Stockyard Hotel (or Horan's), capable of lodging up to 300 guests. The Bennett House, across the way, was a strong competitor. But the favored headquarters of visiting drovers and buyers was the Arlington, over at Central and Watervliet Avenues. The Arlington maintained circus grounds in the rear because circuses used to switch and unload at the West Albany yards.

Once a circus elephant (not Jumbo, as some say, who met his fate in Canada) had to be destroyed in West Albany. His weight had broken the floorboards of his private car while coming in from Utica, and his feet, dragging along the track, had been so badly mangled that he had to be shot. A local rendering plant got the carcass.

The development of modern refrigerator cars sounded the knell of West Albany as a stockyard metropolis. When meat could be shipped in cold storage, there was no longer any point in transporting live cattle long distances to market.

Adapted from "W. Albany Was Lusty Boom Town," *Times Union,* November 12, 1950.

★ ★ ★ ★ ★ ★ ★ ★ ★ ★ ★ ★ ★ ★

Westland Hills and Pine Hills

ON FEBRUARY 1, 1800, a torch was held to the newly installed whale-oil lamps throughout the town, and Albany was illuminated by streetlights for the first time. As Cuyler Reynolds tells us, these lamps extended "at no spot further than half a mile back of the river, the rest of the land being unsettled upon." The city had occupied the Hudson River flats about to their limits and was edging up the bluffs that hemmed it in.

In the 1790s, a flow of pioneers, mostly out of New England, began ferrying the river here and toiling up the State Street hill in carts and wagons. They came this way because the freshly opened lands in western New York and beyond promised a new life and because Albany held the key to the only low-level pass through the Appalacian barrier north of the Cumberland Gap. That was the gorge of the Mohawk at Little Falls.

A perspicacious Schenectady man, Moses Beal, saw how the wind was blowing and started a stagecoach line between Albany and Schenectady in 1793. His coaches left Albany twice a week, charging a fare of three cents per mile. Beal soon stretched his Great Western Mail line on to Johnstown and Cananjoharie, then to Canandaigua. Beal's stages followed essentially the Old State Road, or Schenectady Post Road. It left Albany across what is now the main campus of SUNYA and wound a devious course among sand hills and tall pines, with several taverns as rest stops. That historic road would soon be bypassed by well-financed turnpikes.

The Albany and Schenectady Turnpike, incorporated in 1797, opened to traffic in 1802. The contract called for clearing a road 14 miles long bordered by fences 58 feet apart. With a surface of broken stone bedded in sand, the roadway was hailed as the finest highway in the United

States (at least by the local press). Straight as an arrow, it was bordered by 10,000 Lombardy poplars, which unfortunately did not long survive in the anemic soil. Besides the stagecoaches and much of the "covered wagon" traffic, the pike shuttled waterborne freight overland between the Mohawk and Hudson Rivers. The Schenectady Turnpike was pushed on through the Mohawk Valley as the road which became Route 5. The huge volume of freight alone made the road a highly profitable venture for stockholders for a quarter century.

The Erie Canal dealt the turnpike a grievous blow. Then the Mohawk & Hudson Railroad had the audacity to parallel the turnpike. The company fought back, vigorously opposing the railroad's franchise—a losing battle. There were hard times, but the pike managed to survive and improve. In 1835, "tracks" (continuous strips) of flagstone were laid for wheels, and cobblestones were spread between for horses' hoofs. Thereafter it was known as the "Stone Road."

Of all the toll roads that radiated out from Albany, the most traveled was the Great Western Turnpike, familiarly called the Cherry Valley Turnpike for its initial destination. Extended on across the state, it served as the main route of overland travel to the beckoning West, as well as the eastward conduit for vast quantities of grain, farm produce, and livestock. Herds of cattle, flocks of sheep, and even gaggles of geese, were driven along it. With the advent of the automobile, the pike became Route 20—the pre-Thruway favorite of cross-state motorists, and a popular route to this day with less hurried travelers. Its Albany approach was named Western Avenue in 1865.

The Great Western Turnpike Company was organized in 1799, with Stephen Van Rensselaer, the "Last Patroon," as president, and a number of other Albany stockholders, including the city itself which held 359 shares. Its original length of 52 miles was expanded, and by 1811 it carried a stagecoach line between Albany and Niagara Falls, a three-day trip. The arrival of the stage from the West was always an exciting event for the townsfolk, who gathered around taverns as its time neared. Large stables of horses were maintained in Albany for use of the coaches. Horses were changed and coaches were serviced at points along the line. Enormous warehouses clustered around the lower end of Western Avenue to accommodate the freightage handled by the turnpike.

The road spawned numerous taverns, and before long 50 wayside inns could be counted between Albany and Cherry Valley. William McKown operated the McKown Tavern at the intersection of Fuller Road, in today's McKownville. In 1849, the turnpike was planked as far as Guilderland, but the planks covered only one lane, the other being mostly sand. When two vehicles met, driving courtesy required that the wagon least heavily laden should pull off into the sand.

The first tollgate encountered out of Albany was about where Winthrop Avenue now joins Western, a location then well out in the boondocks. A traveler drove under a narrow cross-roof attached to the house, which was so near the road that the keeper could reach out a window to collect the toll. A gate was let down to bar passage at night.

Along both sides of Western Avenue during much of the 19th Century were prosperous farms, tilling the land later developed as Westland Hills. The famous Albany moulding-sands, in much demand by foundries, were originally abundant in that region. After the sand was stripped off, the residual clay-loam made fertile soil.

An event which foreshadowed trouble for both the Great Western and the Albany and Schenectady turnpikes took place on September 24, 1831, at the "Y" where Western and Madison Avenues come together (long known as "The Junction"). On that portentous day, a "singular looking machine" struggled and clanked into motion, dragging behind it three fully occupied stagecoaches, their grooved wheels fitted to strap-iron rails.

Spouting black pine-knot smoke from its high stack, the iron steed lit out for Schenectady. The engine was named the "DeWitt Clinton," oddly enough, after the Governor mainly responsible for the Erie Canal. This "iron monster" was not a complete stranger, as it had arrived in Albany via steamboat in July and been tested at some length on the rails prior to the official opening excursion for invited passengers. Among the intrepid guests of the first railroad to run in New York State were Governor Enos T. Throop, Ex-Governor Joseph C. Yates, Stephen Van Rensselaer, Erastus Corning, Thurlow Weed, and various state and city officials. Tearful wives fluttered around the coaches, bidding adieu to husbands as if they were embarking on a long and perilous journey. As a matter of fact, their worries were not entirely unfounded. The trip was somewhat dangerous—and far from pleasant.

The coaches were hitched together with three links of chain. They started off with a sudden jerk that flung passengers violently toward the rear, knocking hats off and disrupting their composure. The conductor, or "Master of Transportation," John T. Clarke, blew a tin horn to signal the start, running alongside while the locomotive gathered speed. He then leaped into the car and mounted a high driver's seat behind the tender, which carried barrels of wood. Beside him stood David Matthew, the "engine driver" and fireman. The stack had no spark catcher, and clouds of wood-smoke with live embers curled back upon the passengers. Some of the riders raised umbrellas for protection, but the silk immediately took fire and burned down to the whalebone, adding more smoke and fumes to the chaos. Passengers batted one another with bare hands to extinguish embers burning holes in their clothing.

The cars had no springs and no brakes. Generally speaking, the guests felt more uneasy than honored during the trip. (Thurlow Weed looked back upon the journey as a "terrible experience.") Buggy-loads of onlookers came off the turnpike to line the route, and several bad runaways resulted when horses took fright at the belching apparition. Some wagons set off to race the train to Schenectady (no record tells who won). It took the train 46 minutes to cover the 14-mile track, which would suggest a speed of around 20 miles per hour, a right smart pace at that time.

After the demonstration run, the Mohawk & Hudson Railroad settled down to a daily schedule, the train leaving The Junction twice a day, at 10 a.m. and 4:30 p.m. The round trip between cities, at a top speed of 30 miles per hour, took two hours. The train carried 300 to 400 passengers daily, at 50 cents fare one way. Many rode the train for the sheer novelty.

The Junction remained a railroad terminal for ten years, but it never was the Albany station, proper. The ticket office and waiting room were downtown, at State and Eagle Streets. A horse-car hauled passengers out to Western and Madison, where Allen Street crosses. The only structures around that intersection when the "DeWitt Clinton" made its debut were a woodshed for fuel and a stable for horses.

It is a bit disillusioning to realize that the pioneer railroad—the beginning of the great New York Central—kept horses in reserve. Between the rails was a pathway for horses to tread, and horse-cars alternated with the locomotive at the outset. The railroad promoters, it seems, did not have complete confidence in steam motive power. Indeed, a horse-drawn train followed the steam train on the first excursion. As late as 1840, the Mohawk & Hudson still had 34 horses in its inventory. They were used to transport passengers up the inclined grades to where the train actually took off in both Albany and Schenectady.

The State Street downtown station was completed by New Year's 1833, and a reliable railroad historian defined this as "the exclusive passenger terminus of the road in Albany until September, 1841." When the railroad announced that it would move its terminus from the head of State Street to the foot of South Ferry Street, an outburst of public opposition ensued, and the Board of Trade protested the change. Nevertheless, the railroad started tearing up the horse-car tracks leading down to State and Eagle on September 22, 1841. A group of angry citizens thereupon organized a stage line to begin transferring about 200 passengers daily to The Junction. The South Ferry Street station went into operation despite the rumpus, and made a handy connection with the South Ferry crossing the river.

All this happened a half-century before a high-class real estate development called the Pine Hills was announced, to center more or less around The Junction where the "DeWitt Clinton" locomotive first chuffed into action.

Adapted from *Times Union* articles: "Albany, Too, Faced Sunset: Turnpike Was Gateway of First Pioneers," November 26, 1950; "Where First Train Started: Pine Hills Was Real Estate Dream," December 10, 1950.

★ ★ ★ ★ ★ ★ ★ ★ ★ ★ ★ ★ ★

The Pine Bush

THE THRUWAY WILL CARVE its broad path through the heart of the Pine Bush. In so doing, it will tap some of the wildest terrain the super-thoroughfare has to traverse—bleaker than the windswept moors of Thomas Hardy. These forbidding barrens are within a few miles of both Albany and Schenectady—their natural midland. A segment of them equal to more than one-fifth of Albany's total 19.62 square miles lies within the city boundaries—certainly one of the strangest "wards" one is likely to find in any city of America.

The Thruway will bisect the Pine Bush, but its traffic will be express. Beyond the point where Washington Avenue will join it as an arterial street, there will be no entrances or exits for local traffic through this wasteland. Nevertheless, the Thruway may have an influence on opening the desolate tract to civilization, and perhaps even to real estate development. Cross-trails that are now barely passable to a car will be dignified with viaducts, and their improvement into real highways is foreseen. After all, the lands now occupied by the Pine Hills and Westland Hills residential neighborhoods were like the Pine Bush not so long ago. Take away its harsh loneliness and it would be a rolling, interesting country, dry and easily drained, the answer to a real estate broker's dream. [That this quality would create a future problem for environmental preservation was not a worry when the Thruway was begun.]

The Shakers once tilled farmland in the Bush—in the far northwest corner of the city of Albany—but it has been godforsaken ever since.

This article was written when the Governor Thomas E. Dewey New York State Thruway was in its initial stages and Washington Avenue Extension had not yet been conceived. It is interesting in its original wording, we believe, as a record of facts and attitudes which helps to explain much of the passion and concern displayed during the Crossgates controversy in the Eighties.

A few farmers still try to wrest a living from the niggardly soil, on the outer fringes, and pay taxes to the city for the privilege. One may stumble upon an occasional abandoned clearing with gnarled apple trees standing sullenly. For the rest, it is land that has been long neglected and just about forgotten by the general public. Its past ownerships have been so vague and overlapping as to make the search of a land title a vexatious, sometimes insoluble, problem. Squatters have tilled the soil for years without official discovery. There have been "lost" lots on which no taxes were collected for long intervals. On the other hand, in one almost incredible instance, the Town of Guilderland collected taxes for quite some time on a lot which was well within the limits of the city of Albany.

By swerving into this fantastic region of sand-dunes and scrub-pines, the Thruway will re-explore a locality that was well enough known and traveled long before the Revolution, but which, after then, was elbowed out of the picture by the turnpikes diverging either side, and was almost literally dropped off the map.

Through here, Governor Dewey's wonder road will parallel roughly—in some instances may actually retrace—the ancient "King's Highway" to Schenectady, which in turn had approximated the original Iroquois trail. By giving the main stream of motorists a peep into this weird forgotten world, the Thruway may also set within reach of public attention a treasure-trove of historical lore that has been overlooked (save by a hardy few), because of the relative inaccessibility and unimportance of the territory.

Although the wedge-shaped western arm of Albany is a wilderness in which it is ridiculously easy to get lost, it is by no means a trackless territory. On the contrary, it is honeycombed with primitive roads of horse-cart width, many of them in use, others growing back into woodland. The sand is so deep in some of them as to place an unwary motorist in danger of being marooned. They are ephemeral roads, in a continual state of evolution. The brief detour which somebody made around a puddle, or as a turn-out, may become the permanent road tomorrow.

The very abundance of the trails increases the ease of losing the way, if one is uninitiated. At the same time, they make the Pine Bush a favored haunt for some. Horseback riders enjoy the bridle paths which criss-cross the wilderness, leading to stables around the edges. Gourmets comb the Bush for huckleberries in spring, a succulent species of red-topped mushrooms in fall.

The study of the Pine Bush is a fascinating, if somewhat solitary, hobby. It has been pursued as serious research for many years by such men as William B. Efner, Schenectady city historian, and Vincent Schaefer, General Electric's rain-maker. Mr. Efner is probably the foremost living authority on the history of the Bush, having painstakingly explored it on foot and pieced together its baffling jigsaw of unremembered trails. Why the serious research? Because the bush country enfolds the evidences of the earliest historic travel routes out of Albany to the west. Flint chips and other evidences of Indian encampment have been dug from the sand on the crest of a wind-blown sand ridge which commands a sweep of the entire horizon of mountains. Ruins of the wayside taverns that were the popular rendezvous for travelers and British and colonial soldiers during the 1700s appear along abandoned roadways. There is evidence, too, of the first scheduled passenger train in the United States, which chuffed through here on its preliminary trips.

The Pine Bush itself antedates all these human activities. Geologically, it is the overlay of sand-dunes blown up in the desert left by the extinct Lake Albany. Its soil is mainly Adirondack granite-sand which was spilled into the ice-age Mohawk by glacial streams and washed out into a vast delta. Some of the hillocks, rising as much as 300 feet above Albany's tide level, still tend to migrate in places where the wind has stripped them bare on top. The region was cloaked by a fine growth of tall pines and firs when the Dutch arrived. Indiscriminate lumbering made it what it is today.

Through a desolation that defies adjectives runs a sandy road which is, in effect, the extension of Albany's Madison Avenue. In fact, it is marked on official city maps as Madison Avenue, but out in the Bush, and in the town of Guilderland where it is paved and being developed, it goes by the original name—Lydius Street. Thus a remote and practically uninhabited place preserves the name of one of the earliest dominies of the Dutch Reformed Church. (When Madison Avenue was Lydius Street, city planners projected it all the way to Schenectady.)

Along Lydius Street you may encounter something that resembles an automobile, but you are more likely to meet up with a horse-and-buggy. Only telephone cables, running alongside on poles, indicate that this is 1950.

The Dongan Charter set the west city limits of Albany 16 miles west from the river. (Schenectady's Carman Road—or Fort Hunter Road—was the west line.) In time, the city took to auctioning off lots in that surplus part of its extent, and the city line was sensibly retracted. But the city map still performs a strange gymnastic in that direction, jutting westward in the shape of a tomahawk head. The extreme southwest corner of Albany is 13 miles from the riverfront. The Karner Road [today's Route 155] runs on the city line for a stretch. Embraced in this Pine Bush protuberance are four and one half square miles of the city of Albany. A major reason the city held onto it was water.

Albany had one of the first water companies in the United States. The original private company was taken over by the city in 1851, when the need for an expanded supply became pressing. Patroon's Creek, rising deep in the Pine Bush, was dammed near its source into Rensselaer Lake, more familiarly known today as the Six Mile Water Works. In order to control the watershed, the city purchased surrounding land from private owners to whom it had been relinquished long before. Some of this land is still held in the Town of Colonie. Two hundred acres of it was bought from the "young patroon," Stephen Van Rensselaer IV, who was said to have been "indisposed to part with this valuable property," though the price he got was $150,000. These acres were part of the Holland Farm of the Patroon's Manor. On it had been located the Seven Mile House, one of the forgotten taverns.

The reservoir was dammed near the juncture of the original Mohawk & Hudson roadbed with the modern tracks of the New York Central. The city took advantage of the original railroad survey along the abandoned roadbed a distance of 8,100 feet. At the same time, the Tivoli Lakes, upper and lower, were built into the city water system, down in the North Albany ravine.

The patroons much earlier had sensed the value of Patroon's Creek, but from the viewpoint of waterpower for the mills at North Albany. Presumably to protect the headwaters, a community called Verreberg (for Far Hill) was set up in the Pine Bush. The history books are disappointingly silent about Verreberg, but it is frequently mentioned in Common Council proceedings in the 1700s. It was then city property and was leased out. Seemingly, the tenants seldom wished to stay out the full term of their leases.

What appears to be the earliest mention of "the Verreberg" occurs in 1717, when a lot there was granted by the commonalty to Barth Pickard. In 1718, Isaac Van Valkenburg petitioned the Council for the lease of 8 morgan of land at Verreberg for 31 years for which he was to pay "2 skeple of winter wheat and a couple of fatt hens, and to clear ye said 8 morgan and deliver the same in good shape."

With the aid of Bill Efner's careful maps, this writer was able to rediscover the place where Verreberg had been on the "King's Highway." There stood a picturesque tavern frequented by British soldiery during the French and Indian campaigns. On its site today remains the cavernous cellarhole, with a rank of lilac bushes, gone wild, beyond.

Van Valkenburg, an agent for Sir William Johnson, was an active Indian trader. While conducting the tavern, he is believed to have carried on a traffic in illicit furs. There is some evidence, too, that the tavern was a hot-bed for Tories during the Revolution. Mention of it is found in the report of the Commissioners for Detecting and Defeating Conspiracies, in 1778, when one William Howard was seized and jailed for a robbery committed at the tavern.

The "King's Highway" was the original Albany-Schenectady road. (Any major thoroughfare in those times was theoretically a "King's Highway.") Along this highway were spaced a number of taverns. One was the Widow Truax (or Black Oak) Tavern. At its doorstep the first Schoharie road branched off. There is a bewildering complex of roads around it. This locality, it is said, was part of the land that came into possession of the Shakers. A convert turned over his property to that religious society.

There are wild legends, to match the terrain, about bloody doings in those Pine Bush taverns—of mysterious disappearances, and of human bones found buried in the sand. They tell of the peddler who took lodging at the Truax Tavern, and (perhaps after one too many) boasted of having diamonds in his pack; he was awakened in the dead of night by the creaking of a board outside his door, leaped from the window and ran madly into Schenectady, bringing soldiers from the garrison to retrieve his pack.

There was a period of feverish land speculation in the Pine Bush over 100 years ago. The city had sold at auction 72 lots along both sides of Lydius Street. Known as the "Lottery Lots," they came into possession of a partnership, Yates & McIntyre, who projected a large scale realty development in the wilderness. The properties were re-christened the "Great Lots," and many wealthy persons were involved in their sale and re-sale. The speculation spread far afield, and investors were roped in from other cities. If it didn't start out to be a swindle, it developed into one. Finally, some people who had sunk money in a supposedly flourishing suburb of Albany took the trouble to come and inspect their property. The bubble burst.

The Six Mile Waterworks, long abandoned as a municipal water supply, is now a municipal park instead. The fishing is excellent. The branching bayous make interesting boating. It could become a popular picnic area. Fuller Road has recently been paved as a good cross route between Western Avenue and the Schenectady Road. It may be that

Rapp Road and Karner Road will follow suit some time. The Thruway will cut into the Bush just the other side of Fuller Road, and Washington Avenue will tie into it.

Those "Great Lots" of Yates & McIntyre may turn out to be worth something, after all.

Adapted from "Wilderness Within a City," *Times Union,* November 19, 1950.

PART THREE
★ ★ ★ ★ ★ ★ ★ ★ ★ ★ ★ ★

Supporting Players

★ ★ ★ ★ ★ ★ ★ ★ ★ ★ ★ ★ ★ ★

Hudson and Champlain

BY SHEER CHANCE, two bold explorers—one French, the other an Englishman but in the employ of the Dutch—came tantalizingly close to meeting in the uncharted wilds of upstate New York during the summer of 1609. The Frenchman, Samuel de Champlain, was canoeing southward on the lake which ever since has borne his name. The Briton, Henry Hudson, was at the same time working his way down the Nova Scotia-New England coastline in a small ship called the *Halve Maen (Half Moon),* hoping to locate a passageway through to the Pacific. The ultimate points reached by these exploratory rivals within two months of one another were less than 100 miles apart.

France had been flirting with the vast Gulf of St. Lawrence and its river for close onto a century, and Frenchmen had fished the Newfoundland Banks far longer than that. In 1535, Jacques Cartier, sailing for Francis I, king of France, seeking the elusive channel to Asia, had penetrated the river until halted by the riotous rapids at the site of Montreal. In the early 1600s, Samuel de Champlain began coming to Canada, and he founded the city of Quebec as a trading-post in 1608.

Realizing that the French could never hold out on the St. Lawrence unless they made friends with the natives, he aligned himself with the Algonquins and Hurons of the region. Those Indians were fascinated by the explosive firearm of the newcomers—the harquebus (forerunner of the musket). They were also traditional foes of the Iroquois tribes who dwelt in the Mohawk Valley, and they yearned to see this awesome weapon sprung on their enemies. To that end, they invited Champlain to join them in a sortie against the Iroquois. Anxious to chart fresh waterways, Champlain accepted. A procession of 24 large canoes set forth up the Richelieu River, bearing 60 Algonquin Indians, with Champlain and two of his soldiers with the firearms. The guests wore light armor, metal corselets and helmets. As the river widened into a long, narrow lake, past islands, Champlain marveled at the scene unfolding before his eyes—tall Adirondacks on the right, Green Mountains on the left. Before the trip was over, Champlain resolved to make this magnificent lake his namesake.

The agreed plan was to keep paddling south until they met a war party of Iroquois, join battle, and surprise the enemy with the thunder weapons. As the expedition, skirting the west shore, neared country where Iroquois might be encountered, Champlain's Indians took to paddling only at night, camping under forest cover by day. Around 10 o'clock on the night of July 29, they spotted dark forms on the water ahead—Mohawk canoes going north. The two war parties whooped insults back and forth, but by mutual consent postponed fighting until daylight. The Mohawks landed and put up a barricade. The Canadians, prudently keeping their white allies concealed, spent the night in their floating canoes.

After dawn the invaders swarmed ashore, arrows flying, as Mohawks, 200 strong, advanced to wage battle. With the stage set, the Algonquins parted ranks for Champlain to make his entrance, while his two soldiers slipped behind trees. The Mohawks were momentarily stunned. Champlain took aim with his harquebus and, with a single shot, killed a chief and two warriors. While he was reloading, one of his men fired from the woods. That did it. The Mohawks broke and fled. Champlain's Indians gave chase, captured a dozen prisoners for the customary torture, and headed for home.

Gallons of ink have been spilled on the supposition that Champlain here made a fateful mistake; that the Iroquois he fired upon were so embittered that they became implacable foes of the French for all time. This was not entirely true, as history demonstrates. But one thing Champlain did accomplish that morning was to kindle in the Iroquois a keen desire for firearms of their own. Within a relatively few years they would have neighbors willing to accommodate them—the Dutch on the Hudson River.

In the meanwhile, the widely experienced English explorer, Henry Hudson, navigating a Dutch-owned vessel, had crossed the Atlantic and was feeling his way toward a destination he had not anticipated. Hudson's probing was influenced by letters and maps from his friend, Captain John Smith, commander of the recently founded Virginia colony at Jamestown. The captain had explored to the head of Chesapeake Bay where Indians had told him of a "big water" in the northwest distance which, he guessed, might be the Pacific but probably referred to the Great Lakes. No European as yet had any conception of the width of North America. Smith advised Hudson to investigate the coast between the bay and French Canada, looking for a possible way through.

Little is known of Henry Hudson as a person, and no portrait has ever turned up. Seemingly he came of a seagoing family. An earlier Henry Hudson, mentioned in 1555, was a "man of large wealth and influence," one of the founders of the Muscovy Company originated for trading with Russia. A bit later one Christopher Hudson made voyages both to Russia and Brazil. There was a Thomas Hudson in 1583 who consulted with Captain John Davis relative to searching for a northwest passage to The Indies (Davis was to pin his name on Davis Strait).

It appears that our Henry Hudson knew John Davis and may have sailed with him. The "furious overfall" described by Davis, which had turned him back in Davis Strait, became an obsession with Hudson, who wrote to the Rev. Richard Hakluyt: "There, I know, lies the sure path to the Indies. . . . Be it by Northern path or western, I would that my name be carved in the tablets of the sea." Hakluyt, Archdeacon of Westminster, held high repute as a geographer, and it was he who recommended Hudson to the Muscovy Company when it resolved to try for a shortcut to the Orient by way of the arctic. At a meeting of the company's factors in London, Hudson was proposed for the enterprise. "He is an experienced sea-pilot," say the minutes, "and he has in his possession secret information that will enable him to find the northeast passage."

Evidently, Henry Hudson was a prosperous man. His home was a fine, narrow, three-story brick house near the Tower of London, in a well-to-do neighborhood. His family consisted of his wife, Katherine; three grown sons, John, Oliver, and Richard; and they afforded a maid-servant.

A personality sketch of Hudson may be pieced together from fragmentary comments, mainly in letters of people who knew him. One wrote that "He is as fair as any citizen of Leyden or Amsterdam." Another: "His appetite is prodigious, but he is so thin that his bones near burst through his skin." He was depicted as both "shy and aloof" and "courageous and daring." He was moody and had a "razor-edged" temper. He spent much time alone, avoiding crowds and adulation. He refused to "curry favor" with King James I. Overall, he was intellectual, and exploration was his grand passion.

A theory had been hovering around for some time that the Polar

Sea might be open water during summer months because the 24-hours of sun could melt the ice. It fell to Hudson's lot to demolish this far-fetched idea. The Muscovy Company, bent on finding a shortcut to the Orient, backed an attempt by Hudson in 1607 to sail directly across the North Pole. He reached latitude 81°, the farthest north anyone had yet gone, but was blocked by a solid barrier of ice between Spitsbergen and Greenland. The company sent him out the next year to seek a northeast passage via the arctic coast of Siberia, but he was turned back by pack-ice at the islands of Nova Zembla (Novaya Zemlya). The Muscovy Company at that point became more interested in the whales Hudson had encountered in northern waters than in further icy voyages. Therefore Hudson had time on his hands.

The seven United Provinces of the Netherlands, still embroiled in their long war to shake off Spanish rule, had emerged as the foremost maritime power of Europe. Chafing at the rigid monopoly of the East Indies spice trade claimed by Spain and Portugal, Dutch sea-dogs resolved to go after it in defiance. In 1602, the States General of the Netherlands chartered a powerful commercial society, the Dutch East India Company. A 12-year truce with Spain signed in 1609 gave this company a freer hand to compete for sea routes. Henry Hudson had won renown for his arctic voyages. At liberty in 1608, he was visited by Emanuel Van Meteren, the Dutch consul at London and representative of the Dutch East India Company. The consul told him that the East India Company had posted an offer of 2500 gold florins reward to anyone who discovered a new route to the Orient. Van Meteren invited him to dinner and confided that he had influential friends in Amsterdam who believed in Hudson's abilities and would like to talk with him. Hudson accepted the invitation and crossed to Holland for a conference.

The upshot was a contract with the Dutch financiers, specifically for another stab at a "North-east passage around by the north side of Nova Zembla." If this should fail, then he was ordered to return to Amsterdam for further instructions. Evidently Hudson had already given up on that arctic route and had in mind a western transatlantic voyage from the outset. Obviously, the Dutch company suspected this, hence the stipulation to return to port before tackling any other route. Hudson deliberately disobeyed the letter of the contract, but with sound reason. After his previous pass at Nova Zembla in 1608, he said he was "resolved to use all meanes I could to sayle to the north-west" and to find the "furious overfall" which had been reported by Captain John Davis when he explored Davis Strait.

The contract clause, "Another route would be the subject of consideration for another voyage," suggests a doubt in the minds of the directors. Perhaps in his final instructions (not preserved), Hudson was left some leeway to exercise his own judgment in case he was balked by ice. At all events, no charges of insubordination were brought against him.

The Amsterdam Chamber contracted to equip "a small vessel or yacht of about 30 lasts [60 tons] burthen." This was, to say the least, a pitifully small craft for so dangerous a journey, especially amid arctic ice-floes and gales. A modest provision was made for his family if he failed to return within a year. If Hudson should happen to find the passage, the company promised to reward him "for his dangers, trouble and knowledge, in their discretion." If voyaging was then to be continued, it was agreed that Hudson would then take up residence in Holland "with his wife and children," and enter the employ of the company.

The *Half Moon* weighed anchor on April 6, 1609, with a mixed crew of Dutch and English, and rounded the North Cape of Norway on May 5. Between that date and May 19, there was no entry in the log, hence no explanation of what happened in the interim. Sailors later said they ran into heavy ice preventing further progress; also that some had been in the East Indies service and "could ill endure the cold." The story goes that Hudson then gave his crew a choice of two alternatives: to go on Latitude 40° as recommended by Captain John Smith, to the coast of America; or northwest skirting Greenland into Davis Strait. The men voted for the southerly route, and the chances are that Hudson leaned that way, as he had Smith's charts along in his cabin. Certainly no one in the crew relished going back to Amsterdam so quickly, empty-handed.

In short, the *Half Moon* doubled back to the Faeroes where she topped off her water casks, then set forth boldly westward June 1. At the Newfoundland Banks they saw several French and Portuguese fishing ships at work, and paused among them to stock up with codfish. On July 12 they sighted the south coast of Nova Scotia, where friendly Indians shoved out to trade, who spoke some words of French. Next day they were in Penobscot harbor to replace a damaged mast, and by August 3 they were going ashore on the north curve of Cape Cod, having met a dead end. Thence Hudson cut a tangent straight for the Virginia capes, and the *Half Moon* cruised offshore from the mouth of the James River to ride out a storm August 18–26.

Hudson's plan was then to examine a virtually unknown northward stretch of coast. On August 29 he poked into the open door of Delaware Bay, finding it too shallow with sand to lead anywhere. September 2 they were seeing the "drowned land" of Barnegat Bay, New Jersey, behind its barrier beach. Rounding the tip of Sandy Hook and, having felt carefully into the embayment of Perth Amboy, they then crept up the hilly shore of Staten Island, and Robert Juet, the mate, wrote into his log the famous comment: "This is a very good Land to fall with, and a pleasant Land to see."

Now the *Half Moon* was in Lower New York Bay. Before entering the Upper Bay, Hudson would play it cautious, though he must have been familiar with the 1534 report by Giovanni de Verrazano to the French King, of having rowed inside The Narrows and finding "a very beautiful lake" through which "a very great river" flowed to the sea. At any rate, Hudson ordered the ship's boat into The Narrows to take soundings, and one of the crewmen, John Coleman, was killed with an arrow in his throat. At last, on September 11, the *Half Moon* ventured through The Narrows into the Upper Bay and there found "a very good Harbour for all windes." The following day she dropped anchor off The Battery (Manhattan's south tip).

Favoring winds gave good time up the river, and they anchored near West Point on September 14. The Palisades and the steep-sided gorge through the Hudson Highlands must have thrilled Hudson, who assuredly knew of how Magellan had persevered between high rock walls to get through the Straits of Magellan to the Pacific. Disillusion may have begun to set in when they ran out of salt water above Newburgh. The river Indians proved amiable enough so that the "Master's Mate" accepted the invitation of an old chieftain to go ashore near Castleton and dine with him on a roasted "fat dog."

The *Half Moon* spent four days at anchor near Albany, where shoal water halted progress. Most likely this anchorage was off the mouth of the Normanskill, as an Indian village was located there and a steady visitation between ship and shore went on, with some trading. During the stay, Hudson sent the boat on upstream to a place where they "found it to be at an end for shipping to goe in." This was doubtless the confluence of the Mohawk at Waterford.

The ship commenced the return voyage on September 24, and promptly ran aground twice on shoals. By this time the denizens of the lower river had worked up a degree of hostility. Near Stony Point, an Indian stole some loot through a porthole and Hudson personally shot him. At Spuyten Duyvil there was a running fight with savages who swarmed out in canoes and quite a number of them were killed. John Coleman was avenged.

On October 4 the *Half Moon* passed through The Narrows outward bound and set top-sails for home. Henry Hudson bade farewell to the river he certainly was not the first to find, but which he had unwittingly opened for a flood of civilization. Less the egotist than Champlain, he did not presume to name it for himself. He called it simply the "River of the Mountains."

The river was of no further use to him. His thoughts were now bent on Davis Strait as his next target. Thus late in the season, he figured to save time by wintering in either Ireland or England, forwarding his report to Holland and expecting ready approval of his extended plan. The vessel hove into port at Dartmouth, Devonshire, on November 7.

Despite a caution to his crew, some word of what Hudson had found leaked out in England, and the British capitalists wanted back his services they had before discarded. He was served with an Order in Council forbidding him to work any more for the Dutch. The *Half Moon* was sailed back to Holland by a skeleton crew. Hudson's report to the Dutch East India Company has disappeared, along with his personal journal of the voyage.

What happened to Henry Hudson on his next and final voyage was tragic and actually criminal.

In 1610, a new syndicate of London investors shipped Hudson forth on the Davis Strait expedition he so much craved. His son, John, accompanied this trip. The ship, *Discovery,* survived the perils of icebergs and the "furious overfall," and found her way into the immense and frigid Hudson Bay, which he felt sure would lead to the "northwest passage." After exploring along the western perimeter of the bay, they were forced to make winter camp on James Bay, its southern appendage. After a hard winter, a mutiny broke out against any further exploring, which Hudson insisted on doing. The mutineers set Hudson, his son John, and seven loyal seamen adrift in a shallop and sailed off and left them. Robert Juet was one of the mutineers, and knew enough of navigation to steer them home. When the story came out, the men who did it somehow escaped hanging, though mutiny at sea was a capital crime.

The fate of Henry Hudson remains a mystery.

Adapted from "Explorers," *Times Union,* September 20, 1964, Special Supplement.

★ ★ ★ ★ ★ ★ ★ ★ ★ ★ ★ ★ ★ ★

The Patroons

THE NEW LAND WAS wild and fraught with unguessed dangers. It was not a simple thing to find families willing to tame it and till its soil. So dense was the forest that a squirrel might have traveled from the Hudson River to Lake Erie by hopping from bough to bough.

Fur traders were at best transient fortune-seekers. When the Dutch West India Company was chartered in 1621 as an investment in America (and also to compete with Spain), one of its stated objectives was to "promote the populating of Dutch and uninhabited regions."

The Dutch Republic, having so lately shaken off the Spanish yoke, was the most liberty-loving soil to be found in Europe. It was ruled by an assembly, the States General, and served as a haven for refugees from political and religious persecution. Among those who sought its shelter were Puritans from England, Huguenots from France, and Walloons from Belgium and Luxembourg. The Walloons, who spoke French, had requested permission of the British to settle at the colony of Jamestown in Virginia. Their request had been denied. The West India Company, casting about for settlers to colonize the region above the mouth of the Mauritius River, heard about the Walloons' wish to go to America and offered them the opportunity. The Walloons accepted. In March, 1624, a ship called the *New Netherland,* skippered by Captain Cornelis Jacobsen May, set sail from Amsterdam. Aboard were thirty families of Walloons with enough household effects to establish a beachhead in the wilderness. They had the comfort of knowing that the Indians were already on a friendly footing with the Dutch traders.

The Walloons might never have come up the river. At anchor in the bay at Manhattan rode an armed French vessel. Lying watchfully nearby was a small Dutch yacht, the *Mackerel.* The French captain proclaimed he was there to plant the flag of France because the river belonged to his nation by right of Verazzano's discovery. Captain May disputed the matter. The Frenchman, prudently noting that the combined fire-power of the *New Netherland* and the *Mackerel* offset his own, decided to sail away. And so Captain May brought his cargo safely upriver. After a pause at Fort Nassau, he looked beyond for a fertile site. About where Madison Avenue now meets the riverfront, he put the Walloons ashore. They lost no time in clearing lots, building huts, and planting crops, including Indian maize. At the same time their Dutch escorts erected a small fortress for their protection, calling it Fort Orange—in tribute to Prince Maurice of Orange, liberator of the Netherlands. Captain May (who on earlier voyages lent his name to Cape May) remained for a time to supervise the colony.

A year later, two ships returned, bringing six more families, several unmarried people, and an assortment of livestock and agricultural implements. Some were dropped off at Manhattan Island; others continued up to Fort Orange.

The crops grew and the Indians proved amiable. But then the Mohawks took the warpath against the Mahicans, the river neighbors of Fort Orange. The Dutch garrison commander made the error of sending out some soldiers to help the Mahicans. Three Dutchmen were killed and one of these was roasted and eaten at the spot by the Mohawks. The Walloons were aghast. Not before had they seen this savage side of the native residents. Most of them hurriedly pulled up stakes and moved downriver to join the Manhattan colony. Thus a fresh problem confronted the States General. The settlement on the upper Hudson had been reduced again to a fort. The solution they adopted gave rise to the concept of patroonship and to the Van Rensselaer family dynasty.

The States General in 1629 acted to make a large grant of land to any person who would found and support a settlement of at least 50 people. Such a person would be a Patroon (or patron). Manhattan Island was reserved for the West India Company.

Kiliaen Van Rensselaer of Amsterdam was a financier and diamond merchant, also a director of the West India Company. He applied for a patroonship and received a grant in the locality of Fort Orange. This became the "colonie" of Rensselaerswyck (hence today's town of Colonie).

Five Patroons were registered, other grants being along the Connecticut River, the Delaware River, and in New Jersey. It is testimony to the sagacity of Van Rensselaer that Rensselaerswyck was the only patroon "colonie" to survive.

The first party of settlers came in 1630. Few of them were Dutch.

Dutch farmers were content at home. Instead, much of the pioneer population of Rensselaerswyck included Swedes, Norwegians, Scotsmen, Irish, Danes, and Germans. It was not a bad way for footloose people to get a start in a new land. The Patroon paid for their passage, built their homes and barns, supplied their implements, seed, horses, cattle—even food at the outset. In return they were to pay him a certain rent once they were established. A large investment, obviously, was required of the patroon. Kiliaen Van Rensselaer could not look forward to any return on that investment during his lifetime.

Kiliaen never set foot personally on his domain. He sent over his great-nephew, Arent Van Curler, as his agent. The Patroon was granted a tract measuring 24 miles north and south of Fort Orange along each side of the river and 24 miles deep. Before his death, he owned almost a million acres, encompassing all of Albany and Rensselaer counties and the north part of Columbia County. Under the terms, he had to buy the land from the Indians. No record shows what price he paid, but it is perhaps a safe guess that it was proportionate to the $24 Pieter Minuit paid for Manhattan.

The Patroon, in 1642, ordered a house built on the east side of the river opposite Fort Orange, and it gave rise to Fort Crailo, named for Van Rensselaer's home in Gelderland (Crailo meant "Crow's Woods"). The house was for a minister he sent over, and Van Rensselaer made it clear he then wished his main settlement to be on that side. After his death in 1644, the focus was shifted to the west shore, while Fort Crailo remained on the east. Peter Stuyvesant named it Beverwyck in 1652.

British war vessels in 1664 captured both New Amsterdam (Manhattan) and Beverwyck without firing a shot. The latter was renamed Albany, and—except for a brief interval when the Dutch recaptured it and called it Willemstadt—Albany it has been ever since.

The Patroon's domain fitted in well with the English manorial system. Under British rule it was perpetuated as a manor. Other great manors were granted up and down the river by the English governors, the basis of the landed aristocracy of the Hudson Valley. But the Van Rensselaer Manor was the largest of them all.

Second in size was Livingston Manor, of lower Columbia County. Robert Livingston appeared on the Albany scene around 1675. He was the son of a Scottish clergyman who had been forced to live in exile in Holland, and Robert had therefore learned to speak Dutch. This talent stood him in good stead when he came to America. He was able to make his way among the Dutch of Albany, getting into public offices and marrying the widow of a Van Rensselaer who chanced also to be the sister of Peter Schuyler. Livingston realized that ownership of land was the best way to found a fortune in the New World, and he set out to acquire a manor of his own. By a grant from Governor Thomas Dongan, he was authorized to purchase land from the Indians along Roeloff Jansen's Kill, to the extent of 2,600 acres. When his holdings were surveyed years later, they had somehow expanded to 160,000 acres.

The "Last Patroon," who presided over the Van Rensselaer Manor during and after the Revolution, was General Stephen Van Rensselaer. He had titular ownership of 1,397 tenant farms in Albany County, and of 1,600 in Rensselaer County. Thousands of acres of Patroon land in the rocky Helderbergs never had been cleared. Van Rensselaer decided to develop it, and offered special inducements to veterans of the Revolution who would clear and till farms on that land. No rent would be required of them for the first seven years. He offered the same terms of hardscrabble land in the back hills of Rensselaer County. Many responded. After clearing the uncooperative lands and coaxing crops out of them, farmers came to consider the soil their own. They fell behind in their rents, and the Patroon was lenient about their debts. By the time of his death, the farmers were in arrears to a total of $400,000.

The annual rent payment was supposed to be 10 to 14 bushels of wheat per 100 acres, plus "four fat hens" and one day's service of a man, horse, and wagon. The payment seldom amounted to more than $25 in cash value. Moreover, in practice, the poultry and labor were generally commuted to a load of wood per year, delivered at the Manor House, or a cash payment of $2.

The manorial rent system culminated in the "Helderberg War," which in turn escalated into the Anti-Rent Wars of the 1840s, spreading over seven counties.

Sporadic rebellions against the collection of rents had occurred before, in Ulster, Delaware, and Sullivan Counties, and even against the Holland Land Company in western New York. A sheriff sent to enforce collection was killed in 1791. But the big trouble began when Patroon Stephen Van Rensselaer III died in 1839. His will divided his estate between two sons—the West Manor to Stephen IV, the East Manor to William Patterson Van Rensselaer. The sons set out to collect the back rents.

The farmers refused to pay. When sheriff's deputies were dispatched to the Helderbergs to serve papers, they were resisted, sometimes manhandled, and ultimately one was tarred and feathered and sent back down the road in a wagon. The farmers adopted a practice of blowing tin dinner horns to warn each other that a Patroon's agent was coming. As the horns spread the alarm through the hills, the farmers dropped their work and gathered at a set rendezvous, often armed with clubs and pitchforks. Rensselaer and Columbia County farmers followed this example.

The Anti-Rent Wars brought to a head the demand for a revision of the State Constitution. A Constitutional Convention held in Albany in 1846 recommended land reforms which were enacted into law and sounded the death knell of the manorial system. There were to be no further leaseholds, but existing leases were not clearly terminated.

A speculator named Walter Church bought up most of the West Manor leases from Stephen Van Rensselaer IV. For many years thereafter, sporadic disturbances broke out in the Helderbergs when his agents tried to collect rents. To this day, the title of many a farm is technically encumbered with a lease-rental clause. Often, in a land transfer, the new owner has paid a fee to get a legal release from the Van Rensselaer estate.

Adapted from, "Patroons," *Times Union,* September 20, 1964 (special supplement).

★ ★ ★ ★ ★ ★ ★ ★ ★ ★ ★

Sir William Johnson

UNDER THE BEATING SUN, the mighty but ailing lord of the Mohawk Valley stood for two hours haranguing 600 Indians in their own language, using their vigorous style of gesture. The Indians, who had come all the way from Onondaga to seek the advice of their white brother in a time of crisis, disposed themselves in a wide circle over the lawn of Johnson Hall.

To them he was Warraghiyagey—"a man who does much business"—the name given him by the Mohawks when they adopted him into their tribe. Now he was assuring them that the atrocities in Ohio had been done by a few bad men, not by the English as a whole; that they should hold their peace.

The date was July 11, 1774, and Sir William Johnson was aged 59, erect and sturdy of appearance. But the musket ball was still in his hip from the Battle of Lake George nearly 20 years past, and he could no longer ride. He was subject to a recurrent abdominal ailment, and his Mohawk friends had carried him on a litter through the forest to the High Rock Spring of Saratoga to be healed by the "Magic Water;" again he had journeyed to the mineral spring of New Lebanon.

While he spoke on the landscaped grounds of Johnson Hall, he felt an attack of his old illness coming on. With Indian-like stoicism, he talked on, disdaining to show weakness. At last his legs would no longer support him and Warraghiyagey had to accept help to reach the house—after ordering pipes, tobacco, and liquor for his many guests.

Indoors, he took stimulant, sat in an arm-chair, leaned back, and presently died. The Indians set up a wail of mourning that could be heard afar. Lithe-limbed runners sped into the west to carry the tidings to all Iroquois tribes. . . . Never again would they find a champion like Warraghiyagey. The bell that tolled for him, if they but knew, also tolled for them.

It is almost trite to remark that Sir William Johnson chose an astute time to quit the scene. One of the tantalizing "ifs" of history has been: what if Johnson had not died when he did, on the very eve of the Revolution? Would he have remained steadfast to the British Crown which had conferred upon him—an upstart Irishman of the wilderness frontier—a title of nobility? Probably yes. In which case, might his continued leadership of the Indians have tipped the scales of war the other way?

Fate spared him the decision, leaving him an authentic American hero—as he was a very significant maker of America. By so doing, fate also left his baronial mansion, Johnson Hall, untainted—even though his son, Sir John Johnson, was its Tory master for a brief time before fleeing to Canada and helping to lead vicious raids against the Mohawk Valley.

Once a mecca and rallying point for the Iroquois who trusted Warraghiyagey above all other whites, Johnson Hall is another kind of magnet today. It ranks as one of New York State's top historic attractions.

Pacing the popularity of the Hall has been a growing appreciation of Sir William and his true place in history. Among reasons for his long neglect, no doubt, were the fact that his immediate heirs were notorious Loyalists; and that his domestic arrangements were, to say the least, unconventional. Molly Brant, an Indian woman, was for many years mistress of Johnson Hall and of its master. There is no disputing that he sired many illegitimate children, though the figure of 700 mentioned in London gossip of the day was a gross exaggeration.

Not since the Revolution and the confiscation of his estate has Johnson's prestige risen as high as it stands today. It has enjoyed an added burst from a recent biography, by far the most definitive: *Mohawk Baronet,* by James Thomas Flexner.

"More than any other American who ever lived," Flexner reminds us, "Johnson combined Indian power and white power." For that reason, his role was pivotal in determining whether the continent was to be dominated by England or France. But he never did get along with the Albany Dutch.

Johnson left his imprint all over eastern New York. He founded Johnstown as his personal "capital." He rechristened Lac St. Sacrement as Lake George ("not only in honour of his Majesty but to ascertain his Dominion here.") He built Fort William Henry at the head of that lake. He organized the famous Rogers Rangers. He renamed Fort Lyman as Fort Edward. He was the remarkably skillful colonizer of the Mohawk Valley.

The real "Johnson country" is worth a day of anybody's time. It lies between Amsterdam and Johnstown. The visitor to Johnson Hall, which stands handsome on the rise at the western edge of Johnstown, can scarcely miss other examples of his enterprise and wealth.

The first thing a novice to the Johnson lore will wish to know is how he came to hold the title of baronet. It was his reward for winning the Battle of Lake George in 1755, an event which buoyed sagging British spirits immensely and made Johnson an overnight celebrity on both sides of the Atlantic. It was bestowed upon him by King George II, the sovereign for whom he had just named the lake; and along with the title came 5,000 pounds in cash, and a commission as "colonel, agent, and sole superintendent of the Six Nations and other Northern tribes."

Stupid English generalship soon squandered the advantage gained by Johnson's exploit and almost alienated the Iroquois allies, so often on the verge of going over to the French. Nobody but Johnson could hold them to the British side. Johnson, a despiser of cities, was a master of "forest politics."

Flexner says of his latter-day power: "Boats were named after Sir William, scapegraces pretended to be his relations, sheriffs asked his permission before arresting his friends; merchants were ruined by rumors they had lost his favor; and in Albany, once the stronghold of his enemies, no magistrate was appointed without his approval."

How had a penniless immigrant won such a position in the Mohawk Valley? William Johnson was born in County Meath, Ireland, about 1715, and grew up on a tenant farm as a "poor relation" of Peter Warren, an uncle. Warren held a captaincy in the British Navy, married into a rich New York family, and by speculation got hold of 13,000 acres of wild land he had never seen on the Mohawk River. Warren sent for his restless nephew William, then 23 years old, to come over and act as his agent in turning the land to profit.

This was the open door to fortune for William Johnson. Not content with being his uncle's agent, he conducted a store, got into the fur trade, and took to acquiring land of his own. He especially cultivated the Mohawk Indians, learned their ways and language, and won their confidence by treating them fairly and as human beings. This led to his enormous later influence with the Iroquois Confederacy.

A close bond was forged between Johnson and the Mohawk sachem known as King Hendrick. It was King Hendrick who precipitated the Albany Congress of 1754. Irate at English treatment of the Indians and failure to protect them from the French, he stalked out of a conference with Colonial Governor Clinton in New York after telling him off:

"The covenant chain is broken between you and us. So brother, you are not to expect to hear of me any more, and, brother, we desire to hear no more of you."

This walk-out threw British colonial officials into a near panic and the intercolonial Albany Congress was called in an effort to patch it up. Hendrick and Johnson came and stood shoulder to shoulder. "The most important immediate effect of the Albany Congress," Flexner declares, "was to give wings to Warraghiyagey's career."

Soon after taking up his abode in the Mohawk Valley, Johnson acquired a German servant girl, Catherine Weisenberg. She became more than a servant. In fact, she bore him a son and two daughters. The son was heir to the title, Sir John. One daughter married Guy Johnson, the other Daniel Claus. In some way, Johnson legitimized them before his death—whether by marrying their mother on her deathbed is still a moot question.

A later mistress of the Johnson menage was Molly Brant, who also bore him children and was with him at his death. Tradition says they were married by Indian ceremony. The evidence for either alleged marriage is tenuous.

That Johnson had numerous amours is no secret—many of them with Indian girls as he visited around the Iroquois villages. The Indians took pride in the half-breed offspring of the great Warraghiyagey.

In 1776, two years after Johnson's death, a company of patriot militia swooped down on Johnson Hall to arrest Sir John as a Tory, but found their bird flown. Forewarned, the elder son of Sir William had scampered for Canada, abandoning the vast domain which would have made him a millionaire. None of the Johnsons could show their faces again at Johnstown—or ever be forgiven for their part in making the Mohawk Valley the bloodiest cockpit of the Revolution. The British compensated Sir John for the loss of his property with a grant amounting to $250,000.

All the way up the balustrade of the main stairway in Johnson Hall today may be seen a series of irregular nicks. A folk yarn has come down that Joseph Brant (brother of Molly) made them with his tomahawk just before they all fled to Canada, as a sign to other Indians to protect the house until they could return. They look more like vandalism. The report of Col. Dayton, who led the attempt to capture Sir John, stated that the soldiers did a bit of looting before he could stop them, carrying off some clothing, books, and furniture. The guess seems logical that the nicks were made with a sword by one of the angry looters.

The Johnson properties were confiscated and put up for sale after the Revolution by the Commissioner of Forfeiture. Johnson Hall, with 700 acres, was bought in 1785 by James Caldwell, a wealthy Albany business man, who sold it almost immediately to turn a profit. It passed through various other hands until in 1829 it was acquired by Eleazur Wells. The Wells family kept it until 1906 when the State of New York purchased the mansion and about 18 acres for $25,000.

The Wells family "victorianized" the mansion with porches, bay windows, turrets, and other embellishments which the state removed. The careful restoration program made Johnson Hall as nearly as possible what it was when Sir William was its master.

Adapted from "Sir William Johnson: He Was The Master Of All He Surveyed," *Times Union,* March 13, 1960.

★ ★ ★ ★ ★ ★ ★ ★ ★ ★ ★ ★ ★ ★

Martin Van Buren

THE RAINS AND SNOWS of more than a century have leveled the mound of Kinderhook earth beneath which crumble the bones of Martin Van Buren, the "Little Magician." The passage of the years has similarly muted his image—dimmed the outlines of his sharp-etched portrait.

Oddly for one who left such a lasting mark (some might say scar) upon the body politic of the United States, "Matty Van" came as close as a past President can to being a forgotten man. Viewing portraits of him as an elderly man, one gets a misty impression of a kindly, whitefringed, avuncular, and rather ineffectual old gent who must have made a sweet President. He was nothing of the sort. He was a slick, crafty, Machiavellian politician who "wrote the book" on machine politics, the real founder of the Spoils System, the mainspring of the Albany Regency, the conniver who turned American government into a political game and reduced the Presidency to his own level.

Martin Van Buren, who began life serving drinks to customers of his father's tap-room in Kinderhook, became President primarily because he wanted to be President—and knew how to stack the cards in his own favor. It is curious to reflect that the Spoils System which he perfected on the banks of the Hudson and later transplanted to the Potomac was the same well-oiled mechanism that brought another "local boy," Chester A. Arthur, to the Presidency almost 50 years later.

Still, at one point—as in Chester Arthur's case—the demands of the Presidency pulled Van Buren up to a stature he had never evidenced before. He stopped being the "Red Fox of Kinderhook" long enough to face up, with admirable courage and good sense, to the Panic of 1837.

This one praiseworthy act was not enough to make "Matty Van" a great President, or to offset a lifelong trail of intrigue cynical enough to win him the sobriquet "The American Talleyrand." But it proved that once he put the welfare of his country ahead of selfish party ends, his agile mind was equal to the task.

It also conditions the caricature of the gentle, somewhat lonely old country squire, personally overseeing his Kinderhook farm, waiting calmly for death in that big remodeled mansion he bought for his retirement.

Van Buren's Dutch forebears had settled early in the colony, but had remained totally undistinguished people. Brought up in a village tavern beside the Albany Post Road, "Matty" Van Buren felt his humble station and determined to rise above it. Entering the world on December 6, 1782, in the final phase of the Revolution, he was the first President not born under English rule. He was the third of five children of Abraham and Maria Van Buren, who continued to speak Dutch around the home. He attended the little school in which, years later, Washington Irving was to find the prototype for his immortal Ichabod Crane. The restored building survives today as the Sleepy Hollow School; down the road stands a slick modern school, Martin Van Buren High School.

Trudging along the dusty road, "Matty" carried books for a little girl, Hannah Hoes, his cousin. Years later they married and had four sons, among them the fabulous "Prince John." Hannah Van Buren died in 1819, in Albany. Martin remained a widower the rest of his life. He had her remains moved from Albany to Kinderhook in 1855.

"Matty" left school at the age of 13 and became a law clerk. He studied law and passed the bar. He soon won a local repute as the "Boy Lawyer of Kinderhook," displaying a natural gift for arguing petty cases. Before he was old enough to vote, he was appointed a delegate to a political convention in Troy at which he got the father of a school chum, John Van Ness, nominated for Congress.

"Matty Van" grew up to be an undersized man—only five feet, six inches tall, slender and erect. He dressed immaculately, almost to the point of being a "dandy."

In New York City he learned more law, but especially more politics, at the feet of Aaron Burr. He watched Burr mold Tammany Hall into a potent instrument. When Burr became a fugitive after the fatal duel with Alexander Hamilton, Van Buren grabbed his seat in Tammany Hall. Back in Kinderhook in 1808, he attached himself to the Republican Party of Thomas Jefferson, and by 1812 was in Albany as a State Senator. Here he wasted no time in earning his various nicknames— "The Red Fox of Kinderhook," "The Little Magician," and "The Flying Dutchman."

Martin Van Buren dressed immaculately, almost to the point of being a dandy.

Few will dispute that Van Buren was one of the best political strategists in U.S. history. He "rowed with muffled oars," and lent his name to an adjective, "vanburenish," to define a certain political skill— the ability to be on all sides of an issue at once. He was twice challenged to duels and evaded fighting without losing his honor.

In Albany, Van Buren built a formidable political machine—the Albany Regency—to combat DeWitt Clinton. More than any man, it was he who prevented Clinton from becoming President. He tried to prevent him from digging the Erie Canal. When he saw that the canal was popular, he exercised his life-long habit of expediency, flopped over, and made a show of supporting it. Then he actually turned the canal to the advantage of the Regency by getting control over the large number of jobs it created.

Van Buren's Albany manipulations were too many and varied to detail here. He got himself appointed a Regent of the University of the State of New York (because he had a lifelong craving for scholastic prestige): next, attorney general. He bought a controlling interest in the *Albany Argus,* founded in 1813, appointed his brother-in-law to run it, and made the paper the mouthpiece of the Regency.

Having conquered Albany and made Tammany Hall an appendage to the Regency, Van Buren set out to assault Washington as a U.S. Senator. It worked beautifully. One of his talents was knowing when to climb on a bandwagon. He sensed the rising tide of the "Second Revolution" (the election of 1828) and perceived that Andrew Jackson would be the man of the hour. Attaching himself to the Jackson coattails, Van Buren assured his own future.

A bronze tablet on the National Savings Bank at State and Pearl Streets in Albany notes that Martin Van Buren used that site for the Executive Mansion while he was Governor of New York. It neglects to mention that he was Governor for exactly 10 weeks, just long enough to clean house on Capitol Hill (meaning to eject foes and install friends), also that he then resigned the office to become Jackson's Secretary of State. He thereby set some kind of record by holding three major offices—Senator, Governor, and Secretary of State—within the space of little more than three months. The fact was that he calculated that involved maneuver, his eyes ever on the ultimate goal, the Presidency.

DeWitt Clinton's untimely death in 1828 had left Van Buren the most powerful figure in New York public life. He promised Jackson that he would swing New York for him, at the same time himself running for Governor, if Jackson would then appoint him to his cabinet.

As Secretary of State he won Jackson's complete confidence and became in effect the presidential aide. He subsequently asked Jackson to appoint him Ambassador to England, even though he was well aware that his enemies in the Senate would probably refuse to confirm the appointment.

Sure enough, the Senate rejected him after he was already installed in the London Embassy with his son, "Prince John," as secretary. It was at this time that he met Washington Irving, who was an attaché at the London Embassy. Later on, at a period when Van Buren wished to be conveniently away from Washington during another political storm, he took his famous tour of the west shore of the Hudson with Irving.

As Van Buren had foreseen, his rejection as Ambassador made him enough of a public martyr to win him the Vice-Presidency for Andrew Jackson's second term. This led, as he had also figured, to his own nomination for President in 1836.

Van Buren moved into the White House just in time to have the Panic of 1837 break over his head. Ironically, this development compelled him into his one act approaching real statesmanship. He stood his ground, refusing to let the government be panicked into issuing more paper money, or into rash federal spending to stimulate employment. He proposed the establishment of the U.S. Sub-Treasury, by which the government was enabled to build its own vaults, store its own gold, and issue its own notes.

Nevertheless, in the Whig tidal wave of 1840, Van Buren was swept out of the White House. Five years earlier—looking toward his eventual retirement and coveting an estate to match Jackson's "Hermitage" in Tennessee and Jefferson's "Monticello" in Virginia, he had purchased the Van Ness mansion in Kinderhook, naming it "Lindenwald." Now he retreated hence, to await the 1844 election in which he expected to be returned to the White House. When that year arrived, he made the mistake of opposing the annexation of Texas, and the Democratic convention gave the nomination to James K. Polk instead—adopting the two-thirds voting rule at this point, expressly to block Van Buren.

John Van Buren became a leader of the Barn Burners wing of the Democratic Party; this faction grew into a third party known as the Free-Soilers. In 1848, "Prince John" urged his father to take his party's nomination for the Presidency. By this time Van Buren preferred to grow cabbages and write his memoirs, but he accepted. The futile step was his last political sortie.

From the "Red Fox," he ripened into the "Sage of Kinderhook." He went for horseback rides on the rural roads, and tethered his pony to a tree in the village which came to be known as the "Van Buren Elm." When he drove to services at the Dutch Reformed Church in a gilded English coach, boys scrambled for the privilege of holding his horses. When the church was cold, he covered the top of his bald head with a fur mitten during the sermon. He placed a small observation deck on the roof of "Lindenwald" from which to watch river boats with a spyglass.

Van Buren died of asthma in 1862, much depressed over the Civil War. Governor Samuel J. Tilden attended the funeral, and an honor guard of red-shirted Kinderhook firemen escorted his coffin to the cemetery.

A legend persists that the dashing "Prince John" gambled one night with Leonard W. Jerome, went in the hole for $35,000, tossed the family home into the pot and lost; that this was how "Lindenwald" became the summer home, for a time, of Winston Churchill's mother, Jennie Jerome. More likely, Jerome rented the 36-room house. Adam Wagner owned it for 50 years. Then a Chicago doctor retired from practice and bought it for a summer home. When he died, his daughter, a Mrs. De Prosse, inherited it and used it for a nursing home. After other ownerships, "Lindenwald" has been fully restored and is now open to the public as the Martin Van Buren National Historic Site.

Adapted from "Martin Van Buren is Forgotten President," *Times Union,* October 31, 1954.

Chester A. Arthur

CHESTER ALAN ARTHUR entered the White House under a cloud, a misrepresented and rather pathetic figure. He was President by chance, not by popular choice. Political manipulation had put him in the Vice-Presidency, and the assassination of President James A. Garfield had shuffled him to the top of the deck. People chuckled over his sardonic nickname, "His Ascendancy."

President Arthur was tagged in the public mind as a spoilsman at the moment of angry revolt against the Spoils System (the unbridled political use of patronage). He was seen by many as an unprincipled "city politician" who had openly defied President Garfield while serving as his Vice-President, and was now benefiting by Garfield's death. The assassin had shouted "Arthur is President now!" Most people took it for granted he would reinstate the Spoils System.

But "Chet" Arthur surprised the nation. Never less than a refined and educated gentleman, no matter what his political hue, he rose to the level destiny demanded. A eulogist at the memorial service conducted by the New York Legislature when he died would be able to characterize him as "every inch a President." The respect now paid President Arthur by the thousands who visit Albany Rural Cemetery to honor his grave is well merited; as is the pride which Union College takes in its alumnus who became President.

The President's father, William Arthur, was born in County Antrim, Ireland, in 1787, attended Queens College in Belfast, then made for America by way of Canada. He inched down into Vermont as far as Burlington, did a bit of teaching, studied a little law, then took up preaching in Baptist churches as a career. By 1835, he had a "call" to Perry in western New York. Before long he was back near the Vermont border (Greenwich and Hoosick), then in West Troy and Schenectady.

A Scotch-Irishman of stout character with a "scorn of conventionality and of the fashion which passes away," he married a Vermont woman, Malvina Stone. They had seven children. The second, born in Fairfield, Vermont, was named for Dr. Chester, the physician who brought him into the world.

Chester spent a restless boyhood, what with his family's frequent moves. Schenectady was the first place the Arthurs lived long enough to put down any roots. (The house is still there, at Yates and Liberty Streets.) Chester, who had obtained much of his early schooling from his father's tutelage, was advanced enough to enter Union College in the sophomore class, and was graduated in 1848. While in college he had a schoolboyish propensity for carving his initials. The Union alumni office today treasures two samples—a section of windowsill from the North Dormitory in which is carved "C.A. Arthur," and a table-leaf with "C. A. A. 1848." (Union has other Arthur mementos: a statue on campus and the handsome mahogany desk he used as quartermaster general of New York State.)

Chester's father, an antiquarian by hobby, founded a magazine, "The Antiquarian." Later he published a quaint work, "An Etymological Dictionary of Family and Christian Names," that is one of the curiosities of American literature. He left Schenectady to preach briefly in Lansingburgh, and landed in Albany in 1855, serving as pastor of Calvary Baptist Church until 1863. He took a home in Newtonville at this period and resided there until his death in 1875, preaching part-time at the Newtonville Baptist Church. For a time he kept a boarding-school for boys in the house. It is unlikely that Chester ever lived in that house, but he surely was a frequent visitor.

Chester was elected to Phi Beta Kappa at Union and joined Psi Upsilon fraternity, of which he was made national president after retiring from the White House. He worked his way through college with interims of teaching. After graduation, he "read law" at Ballston Spa, and did some teaching at North Pownal, Vermont, and in Cohoes, where he was principal of the Academy in 1852.

The Reverend Arthur had a friend practicing law in New York, and Chester accepted an invitation to join his firm. Fortune smiled on him. He moved in good society; read Scott, Thackeray, and Burns; and went fishing in the Catskills and Adirondacks. He met and married Ellen Herndon, a Virginia girl who would be his beloved wife until her premature death. They had three children, the first of whom died in infancy.

Arthur had a natural affinity for politics. He served as a delegate to

Chester A. Arthur cut a splendid figure in his fur-trimmed coat, monocle, and top hat.

the Saratoga Whig Convention of 1856 which virtually founded the Republican Party. He so ably assisted Governor Edwin D. Morgan that he was awarded a "gold-braid" appointment as engineer-in-chief. With the outbreak of the Civil War, he did a first-rate job as quartermaster-general, equipping and supplying the 700,000 troops New York sent to battle.

In politics he was strictly an "organization man." He believed in and practiced the Spoils System in which he was schooled. President Grant appointed him collector of the New York Customs House, which made him, in effect, the Republican "boss" of New York City. The Customs House, with more than 1,000 employees, was overstaffed, but no taint of graft or dishonesty attached to Arthur's tenure of office.

When Rutherford B. Hayes, an anti-spoilsman, succeeded Grant as President, he removed Arthur from the Customs post. This touched off a political furor. Roscoe Conkling, a U.S. Senator from upstate New York, had seized the reins as Republican boss of the state. Conkling's machine stood squarely behind the Spoils System and supported Grant for a third term. The Republican Party split into two factions: Conkling's pro-patronage supporters were labeled "Stalwarts;" their foes, the proponents of civil service reform, were "Half-Breeds."

Arthur, a "Stalwart", was utterly loyal to Conkling. At the Republican Convention in 1880, Conkling fought fiercely to nominate Grant again. When the "Half-Breeds" nominated James A. Garfield, party regulars felt something had to be done to pacify the "Stalwarts." Chester Arthur, having suffered at the hands of the "Half-Breeds," became the symbol of compromise. He relished the idea of being Vice-President, accepting the nomination as vindication for his ouster from the Customs House.

Once in office, he evidently had no thought of abandoning his "Stalwart" friends or of turning yes-man to President Garfield. Within two weeks, Garfield infuriated his Vice-President by nominating for his former post as collector of the Port of New York one William H. Robertson, a member of the reform faction. This was a public repudiation of Conkling and Arthur. Conkling's political power was at stake.

As presiding officer of the Senate, Arthur was in a position to fight the appointment. He let President Garfield know he was opposed, even signing a letter of public protest. The two Senators from New York, Conkling and Platt, then pulled a historic boner: they resigned their seats in protest, complaining loudly that Garfield had violated the unwritten law of "senatorial courtesy." Conkling, confident it would be only a gesture, sure that the Legislature would reappoint the pair to fill out their own unexpired terms, put his political career on the line.

Vice-President Arthur packed his bag and came to Albany to exert his influence in their behalf. While he was here, Charles Guiteau shot President Garfield, proclaiming "Arthur is President!"

The nation at large considered Conkling the real villain in Garfield's assassination, and a goodly measure of indignation rubbed off on Arthur. People feared that Conkling would be the power behind the throne.

The day Garfield was shot, Arthur retired to his New York home and quietly awaited the outcome. Throughout the summer, Garfield held onto life, winning popular affection for his plucky struggle. Arthur remained withdrawn. When Garfield died and Arthur took the oath of office on September 20, 1881, he was a changed man. He proceeded to cut off his old associations completely, to the consternation of Conkling and his followers. He even kept Robertson in the post of Customs House Collector.

Arthur turned out to be a reasonably good President. He signed the Pendleton Bill, which became the foundation stone of the merit system in civil service. He prosecuted the "Star Route" scandal in the Postal service. He made the first moves to heal the sectionalism which had continued to split North and South since the Civil War. Because of these and other activities, his term became the dividing line between Reconstruction and the full-scale industrial expansion. At the same time, he set about ending the factionalism in his own party.

A widower at the time of Garfield's death, he invited his sister, Mary Arthur McElroy of Albany, to serve as hostess in the White House. She performed her duties so ably that she helped win popular respect for her brother.

Arthur "looked every inch the President." He was tall, handsome, impeccably tailored and groomed. Nevertheless, he failed to win support of the reform element in the Republican Party. And so, with scant hope of a renomination, he did not lift a hand to win a second term. A Democratic tidal wave swept the country, and Grover Cleveland moved into the White House with a record of reform as mayor of Buffalo and governor of New York.

Arthur retired to private law practice in New York. It soon became apparent he was suffering from Bright's disease. He spent the summer of 1886 in New London, Connecticut, in a vain effort to regain his health. He died on November 13. His remains were brought to Albany for burial for a simple reason; the family plot was in Albany Rural Cemetery. His parents slept there, as did his wife and infant son.

A five-car funeral train brought his body from New York to Albany. The family declined an invitation to have him lie in state at City Hall.

The funeral train was switched to the D. & H. and run up to the crossing at Albany Rural Cemetery in Menands. A guard of four soldiers and four sailors attended the hearse to the grave. Public places were closed in town for the services, which were attended by President Cleveland, Ex-President Hayes, and Governor David B. Hill.

Three years after his death, friends took up a subscription to erect the imposing monument in Albany Rural Cemetery and a statue in New York City. The monument, dedicated June 15, 1889, cost $10,000. Designed by H. Keyser, a New York sculptor, it represents the Angel of Sorrow laying a palm leaf atop a huge, black-granite sarcophagus. The sculpture is mounted on a platform reached by white granite steps flanked by two magnificent urns.

Adapted from "Albany is Final Resting Place For Chester Arthur," *Times Union,* October 24, 1954.

★ ★ ★ ★ ★ ★ ★ ★ ★ ★ ★ ★ ★

William F. (Billy) Barnes

SINCE THE REPUBLICAN PARTY was invented over 125 years ago, it occupied the driver's seat in Albany for precisely 22 years. That was under the powerful and, in many respects, notorious Barnes regime. The overlordship of the big, imposing, often domineering, but withal cultivated, Harvard-educated William F. Barnes began in a rosy aura of reform. It was ultimately ended by revulsion of voters against abuse by the erstwhile reformers. The stories of Barnes and those who succeeded him suggest why hard cynicism is so large a part of Albany's political heritage.

The city's Democratic habit dates from the heyday of Martin Van Buren and William L. Marcy, founders of the Albany Regency, which became the powerhouse of the state Democratic machine. Not even Abraham Lincoln could shake the Democratic grip on Albany. When Lincoln was elected the first Republican President, his vote in the city of Albany was 4,993, as against 6,321 for a "Fusion" ticket (Democrats of both anti-slavery and pro-Southern stripe, plus Know-Nothings) backing Senator Stephen A. Douglas. In Albany County at large the vote was: 10,323, Lincoln 9,324. That was the kind of solidity William F. Barnes confronted in 1891 when he first tried to move in.

Barnes had inherited both his political and his journalistic talents from his maternal grandfather, Thurlow Weed, the celebrated "Dictator" of the Whig Party. While at Harvard, where he earned honors in history and political science, "Billy" Barnes resolved to follow in his grandfather's footsteps. Upon graduation in 1888, he used his patrimony to buy the *Albany Morning Express.* Shortly thereafter he gained control of the *Albany Evening Journal,* the paper Thurlow Weed had founded but which had since passed out of the family hands.

Barnes was a political prodigy, soon known as the "boy leader." He became a trusted lieutenant of Thomas C. Platt, the crusty old Republican boss of the state. In 1891, at the age of 25, he took command of a demoralized Republican organization. Drumming at the theme of "honesty at the ballot box," he began putting an occasional candidate into office. Factionalism in the Democratic machine, at that time run by D-Cady Herrick, aided him.

Another factor in his favor was the German element of Albany's population. Coming into their second generation and acquiring some prosperity after a bitter struggle, the Germans gravitated to the Republican banner against what they felt was an oppression. Barnes needed their help to capture complete control of Albany in 1899 with the election of Mayor John Blessing.

Barnes had learned well the strategies of politics, especially the uses of patronage. There was a saying that "every doorknob in the State Capitol had a Barnes man hanging to it." Of course, he was not the inventor of this practice; he adopted that and other "tricks of the trade" from his Democratic predecessors. But he was extraordinarily clever about it. He even won Democratic ward workers over to his side. In the end, this same gambit was to be used against him.

Barnes made a point of being accessible to anyone, in his office at the *Albany Evening Journal.* He embarked on a program of municipal improvements—street paving, new schools, and the like. His monument, so to speak, is State University Plaza, the waterfront improvement he brought about in cooperation with Marcus T. Reynolds and the D. & H. Railroad. (This development is discussed at greater length in the chapter on "Downtown.")

In 1911, Democrats gained control of the Legislature and staged an Albany investigation by the Bayne Committee. This group reported such irregularities as: singular neglect by city officials to observe the law requiring contracts over $500 to be submitted to bid; a reluctance to suppress vice and gambling; a bi-partisan "deal" on state printing; the levying of tribute on saloons and disorderly houses. One paragraph of the report said: "There is in the lower part of the city of Albany a notorious section known as The Gut. This part of the city, in the Fourth Ward, is devoted to prostitution openly carried on, without molestation on the part of the police or other officials of the city." Barnes defied the investigation on the ground that the Legislature was exceeding its authority. The Court of Appeals sustained him. His candidates won the next election by a bigger majority than ever.

At the national level, Barnes came to be the most politically potent figure Albany ever produced—including Thurlow Weed. He was referred to as "the president-maker." It was mainly his influence that got William Howard Taft nominated for a second term, thereby precipitating the third-party Bull-Moose split by Theodore Roosevelt which put Woodrow Wilson in office. (Barnes sued Roosevelt for calling him a "Boss." Roosevelt won the suit.) Barnes was later a key figure in the "smoke-filled room" nomination of Warren G. Harding.

Barnes held to an autocratic political philosophy—that the "equipped few" should lead the masses. He was militant against both women's suffrage and prohibition, correctly predicting the speakeasy era. His unbending views on both issues won him enemies and lost him votes. He was smooth-spoken and displayed the manners of a cultured gentleman. He was credited with being honest and scrupulous in financial matters; no taint of graft was ever pinned on him, personally.

His enthusiasm for city improvements waned with the years. The Barnes organization became pinch-penny. The pay-scale of municipal employees grew niggardly. Other signs of the crumbling of his machine began to show up. A youthful element of "Young Turks" arose, clamoring for a larger voice in party affairs. Grumbling increased over the Lincoln League, an agency that pressured for Barnes campaign contributions.

The arrival of Alfred E. Smith on the scene for his first term as Governor in 1918 was bad news for Barnes. Smith's vigorous personality administered a shot-in-the-arm for the Democrats, especially veterans returning from World War I restive and rebellious. One of these, a young South End fellow named Daniel P. O'Connell, out of the Navy, made Barnes his target. Before going to war, he had acquired a following in the Second Ward as an upcoming Democratic leader, in spite of the fact that his father and one brother were ward workers for the Barnes machine. O'Connell was nominated for city assessor in the 1919 election, to run against the Barnes candidate, John Franey. The margin was so close it took a canvass by the Board of Supervisors to settle the outcome. O'Connell won by 145 votes, the first Democrat elected to city office in 20 years.

Edwin Corning, father of the late Mayor Erastus Corning 2nd, was the nemesis who finally toppled Billy Barnes. Having recouped the family fortune with his Allegheny-Ludlum Steel Company, Edwin turned to refurbishing the Cornings' Democratic tradition, and with it the Albany Democratic power structure. Starting at the ward level, he built with care. In the South End, he allied himself with Dan O'Connell and his brothers as ward workers with political savvy. Edwin Corning emerged openly as chairman of a Democratic General Committee which, in the 1921 election, conducted a lavish campaign of full-page newspaper advertising, proclaiming "a movement to redeem the city from the Barnes machine control." One ad read: "It is not an unfair statement to say that so many departments of the city government have been proven dishonest, inefficient, and incompetent, that grave suspicion of every other department exists in the minds of Albany taxpayers. We must open the books. We must have full knowledge of what the city ledgers show, and they refuse to tell us anything of our own business affairs."

Other events played into the Democrats' hands. A trolley strike crippled the town, and Barnes made a classic blunder. Speaking at a Lincoln Day banquet, he pompously asserted: "Labor is a commodity." The O'Connells and Cornings pounced on this gaff and turned the labor vote against Barnes. Then came the great "Coal Scandal." When a local coal company went into bankruptcy, examination of its books revealed that free coal, to the extent of 79 carloads, had been delivered to a select group of city officials. Barnes was not directly involved, but he could not dodge responsibility for the loose system that made it possible.

Barnes made one last effort to rebuild his fences. He ordered an aldermanic investigation into City Hall affairs. He directed a change in party leadership, bringing a young Republican, Frank Wiswall, to the fore as county chairman. But his gesture toward having the Republicans clean their own house came too late. The voters were up in arms.

The Democrats put up William S. Hackett, a banker of unassailable standing in the community, for mayor in the 1921 election. He and his entire ticket were elected. Barnes groused editorially in his paper: "Ignorance has had its day in court." Shortly after that, Barnes sold the *Albany Evening Journal* and retired with his second wife to a home he had acquired in Armonk, Westchester County. The Legislature voted money for the state to buy his Journal Tower of the D. & H. Building.

William F. Barnes died in 1930 at the age of 63.

Adapted from "Albany's GOP: The Story of the Party's 22-year Reign," *Times Union,* January 15, 1967. Article originally written and printed in 1961.

★ ★ ★ ★ ★ ★ ★ ★ ★ ★ ★ ★ ★ ★

Glenn H. Curtiss

HALLEY'S COMET WAS VISIBLE in 1910, the same year Glenn Hammond Curtiss of Hammondsport flashed across the skies as a star of fledgling aviation. His feat was a 152-mile flight down the Hudson from Albany to New York. In awarding him a trophy for one phase of that flight, the publisher of the *Scientific American* said: "Three names will always remain associated with the history of the river—that of Hudson, the explorer; that of Robert Fulton, the introducer of steam navigation; and that of Glenn H. Curtiss, the birdman."

Reared in the small winery village at the head of scenic Keuka Lake, Glenn Curtiss had come to the fore as a maker and racer of motorcycles. Owing to his superior engines, he was drawn into aviation by Alexander Graham Bell as a member of that inventor's Aerial Experiment Association. Entering the first international air meet at Rheims, France, in August, 1908, Curtiss won sudden acclaim as "Champion Aviator of the World," by capturing the Gordon Bennett Trophy in a speed race around a measured course.

Upon his return, the Hudson-Fulton Commission, set up to celebrate the anniversaries of Hudson's and Fulton's historic voyages, engaged Curtiss for some exhibition flights at Governors Island in New York Harbor. Wilbur Wright was on a similar contract. The *New York World* posted a prize of $10,000 for a flight, by whatever means, from New York to Albany during the Hudson-Fulton celebration. Two dirigible balloons tried, but failed, and the year ended with the prize unclaimed.

Curtiss made a poor showing at Governors Island because his business partner, without his sanction, had committed the Rheims racer for display at the Wanamaker stores, so Curtiss was forced to use a weaker plane. The wind also worked against him. While he got in two brief flights, they were not publicly observed. Wright fared much better. The memory of that failure rankled. When the *World* extended its prize through 1910, he saw his chance for vindication. The newspaper amended the rules to allow a pilot his choice of direction and two landings en route. Details and supervision were left to the Aero Club of America, of which Curtiss was a member.

At Hammondsport that winter, Curtiss produced a new biplane especially for the purpose, with a stronger engine and simple flotation gear in case of a watery landing. Sure that others would be out for the prize, he kept his plan strictly secret. He opted to fly from Albany south because of prevailing winds and open fields for landing in case of early trouble.

On Saturday, May 21, 1910, Curtiss marked his 32nd birthday by giving his aircraft a final test flight at Hammondsport. It was then dismantled and packed in long wooden traveling cases. On Monday the 23rd, the Curtiss party slipped unnoticed into Albany and registered at the Hotel Ten Eyck. With the flyer were Mrs. Curtiss; Jerome Fanciulli, his young publicity manager, and his wife; and three mechanics.

No doubt Curtiss was aware that, the year before, an Aero Club committee had picked a landing place on Van Rensselaer Island at the south end of Albany (where the Port of Albany now stands). The river margin of that patch of flood plain was shielded by dikes behind which stood a pumphouse and storage tanks of the Standard Oil Company. The rest made fertile soil for truck-garden crops. His first move was a drive to the island and a deal with a German farmer for a few days' rental of a grassy field.

That night Curtiss wired the Aero Club of America that he was going for the *World's* prize, then mailed a letter of formal notification to the *World* saying he intended to start from Albany on Thursday, the 26th. The Aero Club snapped into action, designating Jacob L. Ten Eyck of Albany as official starter. Ten Eyck, a real estate and insurance man, was president of the newly organized Aero Club of Albany. The next day's headlines started a ferment up and down the Hudson valley. Albany newspapers awakened to what was transpiring under their noses and sent reporters scurrying to the South End.

Having set his engineers to work assembling the plane, Curtiss took passage on the dayboat, *Albany,* for New York to study the route and its air currents. He was accompanied by his wife, Lena, and the Fanciulli couple. The boat's captain told him he was likely to encounter the most turbulence over the gorge through the Hudson Highlands and around Peekskill.

Overnight in New York, Curtiss conferred with officers of the Aero Club and was glad to hear that his old friend, Augustus Post (secretary of the club) would go back to Albany with him as the club's observer. He decided to make only one refueling stop, and selected Poughkeepsie as the approximate midpoint. On Wednesday the group bought railroad tickets for Poughkeepsie to locate a landing field. They found one on a farm three miles south of the city, in a place then called Camelot. The owner said he would be honored to have his acres so used and would put up a red flag as a marker.

Alighting from the train in Albany late that evening, they were greeted by a crashing thunderstorm. This gave Curtiss a handy reason for postponing the Thursday morning takeoff, as he learned that the plane would not be ready.

The New York *World* launched a publicity buildup for the flight its prize had fostered. Then the rival *Times* pirated part of the show by chartering a special train on the New York Central to pace the flight. The train would permit *Times* staffers as well as members of the Curtiss party to keep abreast of the plane throughout the flight. The train took up its position on a siding at the Albany station and kept steam up.

The capital city was enjoying its induction into the air age and the populace was duly responsive. As Curtiss's penchant for early morning flying was well known, crowds began gathering at the island right after dawn. A local paper observed that "comet parties" in Albany were giving way to "sunrise aeroplane parties." Automobile loads of people converged from a wide radius, and a few families raised tents and camped on the fringes of the field. Hotels were jammed, and the lobby of the Ten Eyck was filled with members of the State Legislature, just winding up a session but lingering for a glimpse of the noted birdman.

The Mayor of Albany, James B. McEwan, dictated a letter to Mayor William J. Gaynor of New York, which he asked Curtiss to carry in his pocket and deliver after his arrival. The letter said:

"On the occasion of the first long flight by aeroplane in this country, I take the opportunity of sending Your Honor greetings and good wishes.

"The great flight, if accomplished, as I hope, will be historic. It is possible, too, that it is but the forerunner of what may in the not too distant future be a commonplace occurrence.

"The speed of this new instrument of locomotion seems to fit it admirably for many purposes of service to humanity, especially in the way of rapid communication. So far, however, no letter has yet been carried by this new means, and I am glad that these greetings between us should be the first."

Glenn Curtiss chose Albany to launch first-ever intercity flight.

In other words, Mayor McEwan was heralding the birth of airmail.

Curtiss realized he had blundered in announcing his start for the 26th. A postponement at the very outset invited comparison with Governors Island. To make matters worse, Thursday turned out to be a beautiful day for flying. Jacob Ten Eyck appeared in the morning at the hotel named for his forebears and drove Curtiss and Post to the island. Clearly, the machine would not be shipshape before late afternoon. Curtiss spent the day coddling the engine and tightening every nut and turnbuckle. The inquisitive public, roaming about, enjoyed a full day of inspecting an airplane at close range and watching its pilot at work. Whenever the propeller whirled, straw hats flew all over the lot.

A liaison was arranged with the Weather Bureau at Albany for updating on the weather. The forecast was promising, so that a takeoff was scheduled for Friday morning early. A message went to a Poughkeepsie garage to have a supply of gasoline and oil waiting at the Camelot meadow. Curtiss left a pre-dawn call, and hundreds of Albany citizens woke up sleepy-eyed to be in time at the island.

It was a false alarm. The morning was gusty, and wind was the bugbear of all cautious flyers. Curtiss peeled his jacket and spent the forenoon tinkering with his plane, while onlookers grew restless and Mrs. Curtiss sat waiting, with a few other women, on the packing cases in the tent. At 11 a.m., Post and Fanciulli drove off to check the Weather Bureau. Back they came with a favorable prognosis which they had barely delivered when a gust struck so fiercely that it knocked down two tent poles. Several times later during the day the machine was wheeled out when a freakish puff convinced the airman it was no go. Reporters began dropping sly remarks about Governors Island.

Having disappointed watchers all day Friday, Curtiss went up in the twilight calm to reward them. A downdraft plummeted him very near to a crash, but he pulled out in time and regained enough altitude for a fair, if hasty, landing. After a late check with the Weather Bureau, he then announced a sunrise start for Saturday morning, left a call at the hotel desk for 3:15 a.m., and instructed Henry Kleckler, his chief engineer, to have the plane out of the tent and ready to travel by 5 o'clock. Once again many Albanians curtailed their slumber.

So certain was he of a takeoff that Lena Curtiss, others of the official party, and the *Times* staffers went direct from breakfast to the train, which crossed the river and proceeded to the rendezvous point. As plane and train were to start neck-and-neck, and since trees intervened, signals were prearranged. When the locomotive was halted opposite, it was to give three toots of its whistle. The plane's motor would then be cranked, and when it was set for takeoff, a white flag would be waved to the engineer from the roof of the Standard Oil pumphouse. The special train was given right-of-way on the main southbound track; even crack express trains, if overtaken, were to be sidetracked while it passed.

On this Saturday morning, the locomotive shrilled its whistle. The pilot was on his seat by 5:30, in his "uniform" whose most striking item was a pair of fisherman's rubber-boot waders with tops that pulled up to the armpits. Curtiss had adopted this outfit, not in expectation of wading, but for warmth: "I had found them the best sort of flying suit available." A cork lifejacket was strapped around his midriff. The whistle blew, the propeller was flipped, the engine spoke. But the white flag was not waved from the roof. At precisely the wrong moment, a flurry of wind sent whitecaps scudding across the river and the pilot cut the switch. The train backtracked to the Rensselaer switchyard and marked time.

About this time the German farmer, whose ire had been rising as unbidden guests trampled his potatoes and onions, came striding forth with a bullwhip in hand and hailed Curtiss: "You lit in my rye field in that trip you made last night, and you've got to pay the damages." A touch of diplomacy, larded with the promise that his manager would reimburse him amply, mollified the man so that he joined the watchers and forgot his crops.

The hour of 8:00 a.m. was set for the delayed start. Again the train chuffed down the track and whistled. Fanciulli had gone off for a final checkup on weather. He came back with news that a strong wind was working its way up the valley, and this caused a second postponement. By midforenoon word arrived that all was well in the lower valley, but a twenty-mile wind had sprung up by then at Albany. The day was a washout, and the Curtiss group settled for a tour of the State Capitol.

An atmosphere of disenchantment prevailed, especially downriver where conditions were now ideal. Newspapers spoke of his "wasting golden opportunities" and "adding two more false starts to his record." A Poughkeepsie paper did not hide its disgust: "Curtiss gives us a pain in the neck. All those who are waiting to see him go down the river are wasting their time."

The chief protagonist himself was "getting as tired of waiting as everyone else," and recollected: "The delay had got somewhat on my nerves and I had determined to make a start [on Sunday] if there was half a chance." The Weather Bureau was highly encouraging, and once more there was the scenario of an announcement, a request for a predawn call left at the desk, orders to mechanics to have the plane ready by sunrise, a telegram to the Poughkeepsie garage. He thought: "It's now or never."

Sunday, May 29, 1910. Piling out of bed at the call, Curtiss, who had earlier said "Sunday always was my lucky day," drove to the island, sampled the still air, saw a clear sky, and hastened back to the hotel where he phoned the Poughkeepsie police station. "How's the weather down there?"

"Fine," came the reply. "There isn't enough breeze to flap the flag against the Court House pole."

"That's good enough. I'm Glenn Curtiss, and you can say that I have decided to leave Albany right away."

After a hasty breakfast, Lena went straight to the train, with the Fanciullis, Augustus Post, Henry Kleckler, and the *Times* reporter and photographer. Two railroad officials rode along, one the division superintendent. For all its four coaches, the train carried only nine passengers, exclusive of crew. With a cleared track ahead, it was assigned the time of the Twentieth Century Limited, which ran on ahead.

No more than 100 spectators were on hand for the genuine thing when it came. Presumably the transients had run out of patience and the local denizens had heard the wolf cry too many times. Jacob Ten Eyck again drove Curtiss to the field. Final preparations consumed two hours. Curtiss made certain the mayor's letter was safely tucked in an inside pocket and checked for the case-watch in a handier pocket. His flying togs, besides the rubber waders and lifebelt, consisted of a brown leather jacket, gloves, soft visored cap worn backward, and heavy motorcycle goggles. For "instruments," he relied on the flutter of a sleeve as speed indicator and smoke from factory stacks for wind direction. To gauge balance, he sighted across the wings at the horizon.

Wheels left ground at 7:02 a.m. Island Creek being the city boundary, the pilot circled slightly north across it, to formalize the start from Albany. Wires flashed the tidings down the valley. In Poughkeepsie the City Hall bell clamored. In New York, people began to group around bulletin boards of the *World* and the *Times,* and in front of cigar-store windows where progress of the flight was posted. Rooftops of apartment houses on Washington Heights and bordering Riverside Drive were at a premium, while the waterfront parks were overrun.

Adopting an altitude of 700 feet, Curtiss headed down midstream, noticing that he could see deep beneath the surface of the water. "It was a perfect summer day. . . . The air was calm and I felt an immense sense of relief. . . . The motor sounded like music." For several miles the aircraft and train were invisible to one another because of woodland. When the train hove into view, he saw heads in the windows, hats and handkerchiefs being waved. He was able to identify Lena when she unfurled a large American flag brought for the purpose.

Clusters of human beings appeared on both shores. River traffic was plentiful and Curtiss could see boatmen waving. White puffs of steam from tugboats hauling strings of barges told him that unheard whistles were being blown in salute. Thirty-three minutes after takeoff he passed Hudson where it seemed that every home had emptied itself onto the docks. At 8:20 the Mid-Hudson Bridge loomed ahead, and he elected to fly over instead of under it. The population of Poughkeepsie looked like "swarms of busy ants, running here and there, waving their hats and hands."

Soon picking up the pier which was his Camelot landmark, Curtiss veered inland over a stand of trees, sighted the red flag, and bounced to a landing on the only part of the meadow which, as he knew from prior footwork, was free from furrows and ditches. It was 8:26 a.m. People came running. The field was no more than 200 feet from the Albany Post Road, and automobiles pulled off the highway to disgorge their occupants.

The train took the Camelot siding, and soon its passengers came toiling breathlessly up the slope through grass and shrubbery. Lena delivered a hug and kiss for her intrepid husband. Kleckler brought pliers, wrench, and screwdriver, with which he rapidly went over the machine.

An ax was brought to chop a few saplings for takeoff clearance. Curtiss awaited a whistle signal from the train when the passengers were back aboard, and lifted into the air at 9:26 a.m., having been grounded exactly one hour. Approaching Storm King Mountain, he climbed to 2,000 feet. Just past the mountain's crest, the plane abruptly lurched forward, tilting sidewise at the same time, and lost a good hundred feet in seconds. Caught by surprise, Curtiss nearly tumbled out. "It was the worst plunge I ever got in an aeroplane." Moments later the machine was tossed and buffeted about, almost beyond control. "My heart was in my mouth. I thought it was all over." By pushing the post forward, he managed to regain a semblance of control.

"Storm King," Curtiss reminisced, was "the place I first learned that air went up and down as well as sideways." Figuring to find calmer air near the water, he let down to 40 feet and leveled off. Even then a gust tilted the plane so that a wing almost touched water.

The engine was kept lubricated by means of a hand-operated oil pump. Ordinarily he gave the oil lever a push about every ten minutes. Going through the Highlands, he pumped oil until a long blue veil hung out behind "like a comet's tail." Before emerging past Bear Mountain he checked the oil guage and found it worrisomely low. "I must have been too enthusiastic with the lever," he thought. Not until the trip was over did he discover that there had been a serious oil leak.

Out of the Highlands he relaxed enough to enjoy the spectacle of the Palisades. Further glances at the oil level, however, increased his uneasiness. At last, in the hazy distance, he could make out the Metropolitan Life tower and the Singer Building. But he knew that Manhattan Island is 13.4 miles long, and that Governors Island is a half-mile beyond its southern end. Dared he chance 14 miles more? The prize might be won by landing anywhere inside the city limits. As the locomotive crossed the municipal boundary below Yonkers, the engineer yanked down his whistle cord and held it until the train turned away from the Hudson into the Harlem River gorge at Spuyten Duyvil. Curtiss peered into the gorge past the rock bluff of Inwood, the northern tip of Manhattan. Less than a mile back there he could see a smooth patch of green which looked like a lawn on a small plateau. The oil situation by now was such that he decided he must get down somewhere. With a wide swing over toward the Palisades to gain a heading into the Harlem notch, he took the gamble.

The green patch proved to be an uptilted spread of lawn behind a mansion built by the late William B. Isham, a financier, then occupied by his daughter and her husband. Curtiss touched down on the lawn and ran up the slope. The Isham son-in-law, Minturn Post Collins, greeted him and helped him get oil. Curtiss phoned the *World* with news that he was down within city limits but would continue on to Governors Island as soon as possible. While he might have rested on his laurels right where he was and pocketed the prize, there remained an unresolved chord. "I wanted to wheel my craft back into that old aerodrome on Governors Island." The fact that he did so prompted a magazine writer to term it "a magnificent sportsmanlike thing that won him the unbounded admiration of all New York."

Returning to his plane, he found it a magnet for a stampede of people who had transformed the Isham estate into a fairgrounds. A police patrol arrived. A rapid survey showed Curtiss he had flown into a cul-de-sac of sorts and that it was going to be a hairy place to get out from. He would need to take off back down the short slope, drop over the side of the butte, and pick up speed with the drop, while steering between the two steep rock walls of the Spuyten Duyvil gorge. Engine failure or a downdraft would plunge him, if he was lucky, into the Harlem River. The self-vindication which was his aim made the risk worth taking. If it worked, New Yorkers could never again impugn his courage.

The Inwood landing had been at 10:25. It was 11:42 when he swooped off from the Isham lawn, gathered altitude, and was shortly again over the open Hudson. After circling the Statue of Liberty, he came down at Governors Island almost on the stroke of twelve, where the garrison was abroad and cheering. Total flying time had been 2 hours, 51 minutes, for an average speed of 52 mph.

After luncheon at the Hotel Astor, Curtiss was escorted to the Pulitzer building, where the *World* generously invited reporters of other papers and wire services to a press conference. Until this moment the airplane which had flown to fame had been anonymous. Curtiss announced that he was christening it, ex post facto, the *Hudson Flyer*.

The $10,000 check was ceremonially handed to Curtiss by J. Angus Shaw, vice-president and treasurer of the Press Publishing Company. It was the largest award Curtiss ever received for a flight.

The Albany-to-New York flight was the event, more than any other, which marked the birth of practical aviation in America. Up to then, flying had been more an experiment and a sport than an activity to be taken seriously. By achieving the first sustained flight between two major cities, Curtiss had pried off the lid. He had proved that an airplane might dependably start from here and go to there. He had pointed the way to passenger flying, air mail, air express, and all. The excitement kicked up by his deed triggered an outbreak of distance flights which stretched ever longer until they marked out the continental airways.

For the twentieth anniversary of the Hudson River flight, Curtiss did a "replay" at the urging of the Aeronautical Chamber of Commerce of America. There were radical departures from the shaky trip of 1910. The reenactment took place on Memorial Day, 1930, from the recently opened Albany Municipal Airport in Colonie, which traced its ancestry from the river flats Curtiss had initiated.

The airplane was an 18-passenger Curtiss Condor airliner, which was attended by an aerial procession including four escort planes. The actual pilot of the Condor was Captain Frank T. Courtney, a veteran of the British Royal Air Force who worked for the Curtiss-Wright Corporation.

Courtney took the two-engined plane up to altitude before turning the controls over to Curtiss, whom he had briefed quickly. Among privileged passengers were Lena Curtiss, their son, Glenn, Jr., and Mayor John Boyd Thacher II of Albany. At the New York end, Courtney took over again for the landing at Curtiss Field on Long Island.

Curtiss had observed his 52nd birthday a few days earlier. Having become a millionaire during World War I through the manufacture of airplanes, he was an affluent winter resident of southern Florida and had endowed Miami with its first International Airport. It was his habit, however, to return to Hammondsport each summer and occupy the old family homestead where he grew up. He and his family went there after the 1930 reenactment.

On July 23, 1930, Curtiss died at a Buffalo hospital from pulmonary embolism following surgery for appendicitis.

Adapted from Mr. Roseberry's book, *Glenn Curtiss: Pioneer of Flight,* published by Doubleday and Company in 1972.

PART FOUR

Bibliographies

Bibliographies

Books

Albany: Three Centuries A County. Albany: Albany County Tricentennial Commission, 1983.

Capitol Story. Albany: State of New York, 1964. Expanded second edition, 1983.

The Challenging Skies. New York: Doubleday & Company, Inc., 1966.

From Niagara to Montauk: The Scenic Pleasures of New York State. Albany: State University of New York Press, 1982.

Glenn Curtiss: Pioneer of Flight. New York: Doubleday & Company, Inc., 1972.

A History of the New York State Library. Albany: University of the State of New York, State Education Department, 1970.

Steamboats and Steamboat Men. New York: G.P. Putnam's Sons, 1966.

Chronological Listing of Selected Articles and Books

Unless otherwise noted, all articles appeared on the first page of the features section of the Sunday edition of the *Times Union*. Until Sept. 1, 1957, this section was called "Pictorial Review." Thereafter it became "Upstate Living."

Aug. 6, 1950	"Martin H. Glynn in 1918 Saw Dream of Deeper Hudson Coming True," F–2.
Aug. 6, 1950	"Introduction of Bessemer Process Made Area Flourishing Steel Center," H–2.
Aug. 6, 1950	"Smith Proved Insects Carried Germs," I–15.
Oct. 19, 1950	"Central Ave.—Booming Business Center: Improved Street Once Was Known As The Bowery."
Nov. 12, 1950	"Railyards and Stockyards: W. Albany Was Lusty Boom Town."
Nov. 19, 1950	"Wilderness Within a City; Thruway May Reopen Pine Bush: Forbidden Wasteland Within a Few Miles of Albany and Schenectady May be Opened to Development by New Highway."
Nov. 26, 1950	"Albany, Too, Faced Sunset: Turnpike Was Gateway of First Pioneers."
Dec. 10, 1950	"Where First Train Started: Pine Hills Was Real Estate Dream."

Jan. 28, 1951	"Kenwood a Ghost Town but Name Still Circles Globe: Mills Buzzed There as the Rich Built Palaces on Heights."
April 15, 1951	"Mohawk and Hudson Railroad Founded 125 Years Ago."
April 29, 1951	"Forgotten Manse of the Hudson: Whitehall Area Was British Army Headquarters; Mansion Burned in 1883."
May 13, 1951	"Albany's Tulip Festival Week Outgrowth of City's Effort to Restore War-torn Nijmegen."
June 3, 1951	"Washington Park Result of Albany Institute Idea: Albany Group Sired Proposal To Meet City's Spiritual Need."
Sept. 2, 1951	"South End Was Albany's Real Cradle: Revolutionary Capital of North, It Was Birthplace of Industry."
Nov. 4, 1951	"Old Albany: New Scotland Avenue; University Heights Result of Dream that Faded Years Ago."
Nov. 11, 1951	"Old Albany: Lumber Brought Wealth; Patroons Gave Town Golden Age."
Nov. 25, 1951	"Old Albany: Arbor Hill Lives in History; Ten Broeck Mansion Gave District Start As Residential One."
Dec. 2, 1951	"Pine Palisades Laid Out Zone of Albany Business Area of Today."
May 4, 1952	"New Thruway to Parallel Forgotten 'King's Highway.'"
Aug. 17, 1952	"Thruway Bypass Shapes Up on Albany Borders."
Oct. 12, 1952	"Dudley Observatory Soon to Celebrate Centennial."
Nov. 23, 1952	"Burial Pits Reveal Indians' Golden Age."
Jan. 11, 1953	"Attic Yields Letters by Garfield's Assassin."
Feb. 1, 1953	"City Host to Fugitives from French Terror."
Feb. 8, 1953	"Albany Democrats Quarreled with Lincoln."
Feb. 22, 1953	"State Owns Fine Hoard of Washington Relics."
April 15, 1953	(Pine Bush Series)
April 16, 1953	"The Pine Bush: Fur Smuggling 'Big Business' in Early Days of Territory."
April 17, 1953	(Pine Bush Series)
April 18, 1953	(Pine Bush Series)
April 19, 1953	"Pittsfield to Dedicate Melville Memorial."
May 7–8, 1953	"Albany's Own Dan Prior's Legendary Feats Recalled," "The Roving Reporter" column.
Sept. 20, 1953	"Albany Closely Linked with Hudson Bay Area."

BIBLIOGRAPHIES 181

Nov. 8, 1953	"Williams College Linked to Albany Area."
Nov. 15, 1953	"New Book Records History of Area Shakers."
Nov. 22, 1953	"Indian Culture in State Traced to 2500 B.C."
Dec. 5, 1953	"Thruway Crosses 'Lost World' Pine Bush," *Buffalo Evening News Magazine*, p. 1.
Dec. 13, 1953	"State Library Outgrowing its Quarters."
Jan. 10, 1954	"Years Fail to Stop David Lithgow's Brush."
Feb. 7, 1954	"Albany Gaily Greeted Lincoln in 1861."
Feb. 14, 1954	"Library to Show Rare Catlin Indian Paintings."
Feb. 21, 1954	"Antarctic Area Named For Obscure Albanian." (Dr. James Eights)
April 25, 1954	"Albany Congress Was 'Cradle of Union.'"
May 16, 1954	"New Era Dawns for New York State Indians."
July 18, 1954	"Tanglewood Gained Fame in Two Decades."
Aug. 1, 1954	"Canfield Casino Now Houses Racing Museum."
Aug. 22, 1954	"Saratoga Mineral Springs Pre-dated Horse Racing."
Oct. 24, 1954	"Albany is Final Resting Place for Chester Arthur."
Oct. 31, 1954	"Martin Van Buren is 'Forgotten' President."
Nov. 21, 1954	"Schuyler, Burr, and Hamilton Closely Linked."
Jan. 16, 1955	"Amos Eaton Founder of Geological Survey."
Feb. 13, 1955	"Indians in State Cling to Vanishing Culture."
Mar. 13, 1955	"Belated Tribute Sought for George Clinton."
April 17, 1955	"Biography Revives Interest in Ezra Ames."
June 12, 1955	"Washington Irving's Albany Ties Recalled."
April 7, 1956	"Men Against the Icecap." (Thule Air Force Base.) *Saturday Evening Post*.
April 22, 1956	"Journalism Here Began in Party Press Era: First 75 Years Were Belligerent Scramble."
April 22, 1956	"*Times* Born in US Fratricidal Era: Two Weak Presidents Added to Catastrophe."
April 22, 1956	"Mighty 1913 Flood Brought Disaster—but Resulted in Control of Hudson River," G-8.
April 29, 1956	"Albanian Pioneered in American Sculpture: Erastus Dow Palmer's Nudes Created Stir."

182 FLASHBACK

July 1, 1956	"Van Rensselaer Heirlooms: Cherry Hill Rooms Given to Institute."
Mar. 16, 1957	"They Patrol the North Front." (The Royal Norwegian Air Force.) *Saturday Evening Post.*
June 16, 1957	"Writers of Our Land: Hudson Valley Disclosed as True Birthplace of American Literature."
Sept. 1, 1957	"Mohawk Village Site Sheds Light on 14th Century Indians." In this issue "Upstate Living" replaced "Pictorial Review." All subsequent essays are on page one of this section unless otherwise indicated.
Feb. 2, 1958	"Teddy Roosevelt—Man of Destiny: Wild Ride Took Him to Presidency." (Article celebrating centennial of his birth.)
Feb. 23, 1958	"A New Picture of Mike Cronin: Daughters Provide Unpublished Data."
Feb. 23, 1958	"Call This a Blizzard? Recent Storm a Flurry Compared with '88."
Mar. 4, 1958	"City of Hudson Once Whaling Port: Founded by New Englanders, Fleets of Square Riggers Roamed Seas."
Mar. 16, 1958	"Fighter for Irish Freedom: Glynn Paved Way for Free State," F-1.
May 18, 1958	"City's Greatest: 28 Names on Hall of Fame Roster."
Jan. 4, 1959	"From Famed Folly to Fabulous Forty-ninth: Alaska Owes Debt to Albany's Seward and O'Brien."
June 28, 1959	"Long Lost Lafayette Letter to Clinton Found: Prized Message of 1778 in Possession of Albany Man."
Feb. 7, 1960	"270 Years Ago: The Schenectady Massacre."
Mar. 13, 1960	"Sir William Johnson: He was the Master of All He Surveyed."
July 10, 1960	"The Beautiful Helderbergs," E-1.
Feb. 5, 1961	"Abolitionists Gather in Albany," A-1.
Feb. 12, 1961	"Historic Copper Plate: Canal Relic on Display."
Feb. 12, 1961	"Threads of Lincoln-Booth Tragedy Crossed First in Albany," A-6.
Feb. 19, 1961	"Lincoln Here: Tracks are Guarded," A-1.
Mar. 5, 1961	"Strange Battle: Monitor vs Merrimac," A-10.
April 9, 1961	"Shells That Rocked Fort Sumter Ended Albany's Civil War," A-15.
April 11, 1961	"Local GOP Chiefs, Paper Changed Tune on Rail Splitter," H-1.
April 16, 1961	"A Tragedy That Blighted 2 More Lives," E-4. (Lincoln assassination)
Aug. 13, 1961	"Brady Birthplace Sought: Photographer Native to Area," F-7.

Sept. 10-22, 1961	"The Irish in Albany." "1st Irishman Here was an Anderson." "Dongan, Fine Colonial Leader, Granted Albany's City Charter." "Act of Legislature Incorporated St. Patrick's Society Here in 1807." "Penniless Immigrant, 20, Became Albany's First Irish Bank President." "Erie Canal Construction Brought Great Influx of Irish to Albany." "Famed James Intellectual Dynasty Got Start in Colonial-Day Albany." "Martin H. Glynn, Albany's Own, Aided Settlement of British-Irish Dispute." "Irish Editors Active in Albany." "Immaculate Conception Cathedral Second for Catholics in N.Y. State." "Dashing Civil War General Has Place of Honor in Capitol Park." "Half of Albany's Population Traces Ancestors Back to Erin."
January, 1962	*Monitor Centennial Issue, New York State and the Civil War.* (Series published by New York State Civil War Centennial Commission; Mr. Roseberry was responsible for this entire issue.)
February, 1962	*Abraham Lincoln Issue, New York State and the Civil War.* (Series published by New York State Civil War Centennial Commission; Mr. Roseberry was responsible for most of this issue.)
April, 1962	"On Eve of Civil War, Legislators Orated, Then Failed to Put Militia into Shape," *New York State and the Civil War.* (Series published by the New York State Civil War Centennial Commission.)
June, 1962	"Ellsworth was 'Golden Boy'; Death Made Him a Martyr of the North," *New York State and the Civil War.* (Series published by New York State Civil War Centennial Commission.)
July, 1962	"State's 'Fightingest' General: Dan Butterfield Put New Life in Army of the Potomac at Crucial Time," and "Taps: How Butterfield Composed Bugle Call," *Butterfield Memorial Issue, New York State and the Civil War.* (Series published by New York State Civil War Centennial Commission.)
August, 1962	*Ulysses S. Grant Issue, New York State and the Civil War.* (Series published by New York State Civil War Centennial Commission.)
Spring, 1963	"Long Island: Cradle of Aviation." *Grumman Horizons.*
1964	*Capitol Story.* State of New York.
Sept. 20, 1964	*Historic Capitaland* 1614–1969 (special supplement). "Fort Nassau" "Explorers" "Literature" "Patroons" "Indians" "Revolution" "Science"
April 12, 1965	"State Capital Ironically Linked to Lincoln Tragedy: Actor Checks into Hotel in Albany," p. 18.

184 FLASHBACK

April 13, 1965	"Lincoln Assassination in Theater Stuns, Angers Nation: Albany Residents Furious with Southern Backers," p. 13.
April 14, 1965	"Lincoln's Bier Visited by 50,000 During Albany Stopover: Boston Corbett, Troy Native, Killed John Wilkes Booth," p. 21.
1966	*The Challenging Skies.* New York: Doubleday and Company, Inc.
1966	*Steamboats and Steamboat Men.* New York: G. P. Putnam's Sons.
Jan. 15, 1967	"Albany's GOP: The Story of the Party's 22-Year Reign." (Article written in 1961.)
Dec. 9, 1967	"The Fantastic Flight of Charles Levine." *Coronet.*
Winter, 1968	"TR's Midnight Ride." *York State Tradition.*
1970	*A History of the New York State Library.* University of the State of New York, State Education Department.
1972	*Glenn Curtiss: Pioneer of Flight.* New York: Doubleday and Company, Inc.
Summer, 1975	"Martha Reben: Wilderness Lady." *Adirondack Life.*
1982	*From Niagara to Montauk: The Scenic Pleasures of New York State.* State University of New York Press.
Nov.–Dec., 1982	"On Wings of Daring." (The Glenn Curtiss story.) *New York Alive.*
1983	*Albany: Three Centuries a County.* Albany County Tricentennial Commission.
Nov.–Dec., 1983	"Where the Hudson Begins." *New York Alive.*

Thematic Listing of Selected Articles and Books

The topics presented fall into the following seven categories:
People—Individuals
People—Groups
Work (Fields of Endeavor)
Places
Historical Events
Links (To Albany)
Miscellany

Within topics, articles are grouped in alphabetical order. If there is more than one article on a given subject, they are presented in chronological order.

Unless otherwise noted, all articles appeared on the first page of the features section of the Sunday *Times Union.* Until September 1, 1957, this section was entitled "Pictorial Review"; thereafter it was called "Upstate Living."

PEOPLE—INDIVIDUALS

Survey
    May 18, 1958 "City's Greatest: 28 Names on Hall of Fame Roster."

BIBLIOGRAPHIES

Ames, Ezra
    April 17, 1955 "Biography Revives Interest in Ezra Ames."

Anderson, John
    Sept. 10, 1961 "1st Irishman Here was an Anderson," A-20.

Arthur, Chester
    Oct. 24, 1954 "Albany is Final Resting Place for Chester Arthur."

Brady, Matthew
    Aug. 13, 1961 "Brady Birthplace Sought: Photographer Native to Area," F-7.

Burr, Aaron
    Nov. 21, 1954 "Schuyler, Burr, and Hamilton Closely Linked."

Butterfield, Dan
    July, 1962 "State's 'Fightingest' General: Dan Butterfield Put New Life in Army of the Potomac at Crucial Time," and "Taps: How Butterfield Composed Bugle Call." *Butterfield Memorial Issue, New York State and the Civil War.* Published by New York State Civil War Centennial Commission.

Cassidy, William
    Sept. 17, 1961 "Irish Editors Active in Albany."

Catlin
    Feb. 14, 1954 "Library to Show Rare Catlin Indian Paintings."

Clinton, George
    June 28, 1959 "Long Lost Lafayette Letter to Clinton Found: Prized Message of 1778 in Possession of Albany Man."
    Mar. 13, 1955 "Belated Tribute Sought for George Clinton."

Cronin, Mike
    Feb. 23, 1958 "A New Picture of Mike Cronin: Daughters Provide Unpublished Data."

Curtiss, Glenn H.
    1972 *Glenn Curtiss: Pioneer of Flight.* New York: Doubleday & Co.

Dongan, Thomas
    Sept. 11, 1961 "Dongan, Fine Colonial Leader, Granted Albany's City Charter."

Eaton, Amos
    Jan. 18, 1955 "Amos Eaton Founder of Geological Survey."

Eights, James
    Feb. 21, 1954 "Antarctic Area Named for Obscure Albanian."

Ellsworth, Elmer E.
    June, 1962 "Ellsworth was 'Golden Boy'; Death Made Him a Martyr of the North." *New York State and the Civil War.* Published by New York State Civil War Centennial Commission.

Glynn, Martin
    Aug. 6, 1950 "Martin H. Glynn in 1918 Saw Dream of Deeper Hudson Coming True," F-2.
    Mar. 18, 1958 "Fighter for Irish Freedom: Glynn Paved Way for Free State."
    Sept. 19, 1961 "Martin H. Glynn, Albany's Own, Aided Settlement of British-Irish Dispute."

186 FLASHBACK

Grant, Ulysses S.
    Aug., 1962   *Ulysses S. Grant Issue. New York State and the Civil War.* Published by New York State Civil War Centennial Commission.

Hamilton, Alexander
    Nov. 21, 1954   "Schuyler, Burr, and Hamilton Closely Linked."

Hastings, Hugh L.
    Sept. 17, 1961   "Irish Editors Active in Albany."

James, William
    Sept. 16, 1961   "Famed James Intellectual Dynasty Got Start in Colonial-Day Albany."

Johnson, Sir William
    Mar. 13, 1960   "Sir William Johnson: He was the Master of All He Surveyed."

Lafayette, Marquis de
    June 28, 1959   "Long Lost Lafayette Letter to Clinton Found: Prized Message of 1778 in Possession of Albany Man."

Levine, Charles
    December, 1967   "The Fantastic Flight of Charles Levine," *Coronet.*

Lincoln, Abraham
    Feb., 1962   *Abraham Lincoln Issue, New York State and the Civil War.* Published by New York State Civil War Centennial Commission. (Also see Lincoln entries in section on Links.)

Lithgow, David C.
    Jan. 10, 1954   "Years Fail to Stop David Lithgow's Brush."

Melville, Herman
    April 19, 1953   "Pittsfield to Dedicate Melville Memorial."

O'Brien, Leo
    Jan. 4, 1959   "From Famed Folly to Fabulous Forty-ninth: Alaska Owes Debt to Albany's Seward and O'Brien."

Palmer, Erastus Dow
    April 29, 1956   "Albanian Pioneered in American Sculpture: Erastus Dow Palmer's Nudes Created Stir."

Prior, Dan
    May 7-8, 1953   "The Roving Reporter column."

Reben, Martha
    Summer, 1975   "Martha Reben: Wilderness Lady." *Adirondack Life.*

Roosevelt, Theodore
    Feb. 2, 1958   "Teddy Roosevelt—Man of Destiny: Wild Ride Took Him to Presidency."
    Winter, 1968   "TR's Midnight Ride," published in *York State Tradition,* pp. 5-9.

Schuyler, Philip
    Nov. 21, 1954   "Schuyler, Burr, and Hamilton Closely Linked."

Seward, William H.
    Jan. 4, 1959   "From Famed Folly to Fabulous Forty-ninth: Alaska Owes Debt to Albany's Seward and O'Brien."

Sheridan, Philip
    Sept. 20, 1961   "Dashing Civil War General Has Place of Honor in Capitol Park."

Smith, Theobald
    Aug. 6, 1950   "Smith Proved Insects Carried Germs," I-15.

Van Buren, Martin
    Oct. 31, 1954   "Martin Van Buren is 'Forgotten' President."

Walsh, Dudley
    Sept. 13, 1961   "Penniless Immigrant, 20, Became Albany's First Irish Bank President."

PEOPLE: GROUPS

Dutch
    Sept. 20, 1964   (Special Supplement) "Patroons."

Europeans
    Sept. 20, 1964   (Special Supplement) "Explorers."

French
    Feb. 1, 1953   "City Host to Fugitives from French Terror."

Indians
    Nov. 23, 1952   "Burial Pits Reveal Indians' Golden Age."
    Nov. 22, 1953   "Indian Culture in State Traced to 2500 B.C."
    May 16, 1954   "New Era Dawns for New York State Indians."
    Feb. 13, 1955   "Indians in State Cling to Vanishing Culture."
    Sept. 1, 1957   "Mohawk Village Site Sheds Light on 14th Century Indians."

Irish
    Sept. 10-22, 1961   "The Irish in Albany."
    Sept. 12   "Act of Legislature Incorporated St. Patrick's Society Here in 1807."
    Sept. 14   "Erie Canal Construction Brought Great Influx of Irish to Albany," p. 35.
    Sept. 18   "Immaculate Conception Cathedral Second for Catholics in N.Y. State."
    Sept. 22   "Half of Albany's Population Traces Ancestors Back to Erin."

Republicans
    Jan. 15, 1967   "Albany's GOP: The Story of the Party's 22-Year Reign." (Article written in 1961.)

Shakers
    Nov. 15, 1953   "New Book Records History of Area Shakers."

WORK (FIELDS OF ENDEAVOR)

Aviation
    Spring, 1963   "Long Island: Cradle of Aviation," *Grumman Horizons.*
    1966   *The Challenging Skies* Aviation History 1919-1939. New York: Doubleday and Company, Inc.
    Dec., 1967   "The Fantastic Flight of Charles Levine," *Coronet.*
    Nov.-Dec., 1982   "On Wings of Daring," *New York Alive.*
    1972   *Glenn Curtiss: Pioneer of Flight.* New York: Doubleday and Company, Inc.

Navigation
    1966   *Steamboats and Steamboat Men.* New York: G. P. Putnam's Sons.

188   FLASHBACK

Publishing
  Aug. 6, 1950   "First Publisher Fled Angry Albanians," H-12.
  April 22, 1956   "Journalism Here Began in Party Press Era: First 75 Years were Belligerent Scramble."
  June 16, 1957   "Writers of Our Land: Hudson Valley Disclosed as True Birthplace of American Literature."
  Sept. 20, 1964   "Literature" (Special Supplement).

Military
  April 7, 1956   "Men Against the Icecap," *Saturday Evening Post.*
  Mar. 16, 1957   "They Patrol the North Front," *Saturday Evening Post.*

Science (See also individual scientists.)
  Sept. 20, 1964   "Science" (Special Supplement).

Steel manufacture
  Aug. 6, 1950   "Introduction of Bessemer Process Made Area Flourishing Steel Center," H-2.

Transportation
  Nov. 12, 1950   "Railyards and Stockyards: W. Albany Was Lusty Boom Town."
  Apr. 15, 1951   "Mohawk and Hudson Railroad Founded 125 Years Ago."

PLACES

Albany County
  1983   *Albany: Three Centuries a County.* Albany County Tricentennial Commission.

Arbor Hill
  Nov. 25, 1951   "Old Albany: Arbor Hill Lives in History; Ten Broeck Mansion Gave District Start As Residential One."

Capitol Hill
  Jan. 13, 1952   "Capitol Hill: Acropolis of Albany."
  1964   *Capitol Story.* State of New York. Expanded second edition 1983.

Central Avenue/Westland Hills
  Oct. 19, 1950   "Central Ave.—Booming Business Center: Improved Street Once Was Known As The Bowery."

Cherry Hill
  July 1, 1956   "Van Rensselaer Heirlooms: Cherry Hill Rooms Given to Institute."

Delaware Ave. (See Whitehall.)

Downtown
  Dec. 2, 1951   "Pine Palisades Laid Out Zone of Albany Business Area of Today."
  Sept. 20, 1964   "Fort Nassau" (Special Supplement).

Fort Nassau (See Downtown.)

Helderbergs
  July 10, 1960   "The Beautiful Helderbergs," E-1.

Kenwood
  Jan. 28, 1951   "Kenwood a Ghost Town But Name Still Circles Globe: Mills Buzzed There as the Rich Built Palaces on Heights."

New York State
  1982 *From Niagara to Montauk: The Scenic Pleasures of New York State.* Albany: State University of New York Press.

New York State Library
  1970 *A History of the New York State Library.* Albany: University of the State of New York, State Education Department.

North Albany
  Nov. 11, 1951   "Old Albany: Lumber Brought Wealth; Patroons Gave Town Golden Age."

Pine Bush
  Nov. 19, 1950   "Wilderness Within a City; Thruway May Reopen Pine Bush: Forbidden Wasteland Within a Few Miles of Albany and Schenectady May be Opened to Development by New Highway."

Pine Hills
  Dec. 10, 1950   "Where First Train Started: Pine Hills was Real Estate Dream."
  Nov. 26, 1950   "Albany, Too, Faced Sunset: Turnpike was Gateway of First Pioneers."

South End
  Sept. 2, 1951   "South End Was Albany's Real Cradle: Revolutionary Capital of North, it was Birthplace of Industry."

University Heights
  Nov. 4, 1951   "Old Albany: New Scotland Avenue; University Heights Result of Dream that Faded Years Ago."

Washington Park
  June 3, 1951   "Washington Park Result of Albany Institute Idea: Albany Group Sired Proposal To Meet City's Spiritual Need."

Whitehall/Delaware Ave.
  April 29, 1951   "Forgotten Manse of the Hudson: Whitehall Area Was British Army Headquarters; Mansion Burned in 1883."

HISTORIC EVENTS

Albany Congress
  April 25, 1954   "Albany Congress Was 'Cradle of Union.'"

Blizzard of '88
  Feb. 23, 1958   "Call This a Blizzard? Recent Storm a Flurry Compared with '88."

Civil War (See also "Lincoln.")
  Feb. 5, 1961   "Abolitionists Gather in Albany," A-1.
  April 9, 1961   "Shells that Rocked Fort Sumter Ended Albany's Civil War," A-15.
  Mar. 5, 1961   "Strange Battle: Monitor vs Merrimac," A-10.
  Jan., 1962   *Monitor Centennial Issue, New York State and the Civil War.* Published by New York State Civil War Centennial Commission.
  April, 1962   "On Eve of Civil War, Legislators Orated, Then Failed to Put Militia Into Shape," *New York State and the Civil War.* Published by New York State Civil War Centennial Commission.

Flood of 1913
  April 22, 1956   "Mighty 1913 Flood Brought Disaster—but Resulted in Control of Hudson River," G-8.

190 FLASHBACK

Railroad's Founding
   April 15, 1951 "Mohawk and Hudson Railroad Founded 125 Years Ago."

Revolutionary War
   Sept. 20, 1964 (Special Supplement) "Revolution."

Schenectady Massacre
   Feb. 7, 1960 "270 Years Ago: The Schenectady Massacre."

Times Union (origins)
   April 22, 1956 "*Times* Born in U.S. Fratricidal Era: Two Weak Presidents Added to Catastrophe."

Tulip Festival (origins)
   May 13, 1951 "Albany's Tulip Festival Week Outgrowth of City's Effort to Restore War-torn Nijmegen."

LINKS (TO ALBANY)

Antarctica
   Feb. 21, 1954 "Antarctic Area Named For Obscure Albanian." (Dr. James Eights)

Garfield assassination
   Jan. 11, 1953 "Attic Yields Letters by Garfield's Assassin."

Hudson (city)
   Mar. 4, 1958 "City of Hudson Once Whaling Port: Founded by New Englanders, Fleets of Square Riggers Roamed Seas."

Hudson Bay Area
   Sept. 20, 1953 "Albany Closely Linked with Hudson Bay Area."

Irving, Washington
   June 12, 1955 "Washington Irving's Albany Ties Recalled."

Lincoln (See also "Civil War.")
   Feb. 8, 1953 "Albany Democrats Quarreled with Lincoln."
   Feb. 7, 1954 "Albany Gaily Greeted Lincoln in 1861."
   Feb. 12, 1961 "Threads of Lincoln-Booth Tragedy Crossed First in Albany," A-6.
   Feb. 19, 1961 "Lincoln Here: Tracks are Guarded," A-1.
   April 16, 1961 "A Tragedy That Blighted 2 More Lives," E-4.
   Feb., 1962 *Abraham Lincoln Issue, New York State and the Civil War.* Published by New York State Civil War Centennial Commission.
   April 11, 1965 "Local GOP Chiefs, Paper Changed Tune on Rail Splitter," H-1.
   April 12, 1965 "State Capital Ironically Linked to Lincoln Tragedy: Actor Checks into Hotel in Albany," p. 18.
   April 13, 1965 "Lincoln Assassination in Theater Stuns, Angers Nation: Albany Residents Furious with Southern Backers," p. 13.
   April 14, 1965 "Lincoln's Bier Visited by 50,000 During Stopover," p. 21.

Williams College
   Nov. 8, 1953 "Williams College Linked to Albany Area."

Miscellany
   June 1, 1952 "New Home Needed: Traffic Isolates Schuyler Statue."
   Aug. 17, 1952 "Thruway Bypass Shapes Up on Albany Borders."
   Oct. 12, 1952 "Dudley Observatory Soon to Celebrate Centennial."
   Feb. 22, 1953 "State Owns Fine Hoard of Washington Relics."
   Dec. 13, 1953 "State Library Outgrowing its Quarters."

July 18, 1954 "Tanglewood Gained Fame in Two Decades."
Aug. 1, 1954 "Canfield Casino Now Houses Racing Museum."
Aug. 22, 1954 "Saratoga Mineral Springs Pre-dated Horse Racing."
Feb. 12, 1961 "Historic Copper Plate: Canal Relic on Display."
Nov.–Dec., 1983 "Where the Hudson Begins." *New York Alive.*

Index

abolitionists, 37–42
Academy Park, 103, 106
Albany Academy, 79, 102–05, 106
Albany & Schenectady Turnpike, 120–21, 122, 129
Albany Argus, 105, 153
Albany Congress, 14–19, 147–48
Albany Evening Journal, 31, 32, 34, 42, 162, 163, 165; building, 83, 165
Albany Institute of History and Art, 1, 55, 110, 111
Albany Iron Works, 59
Albany Medical College, 105
Albany Morning Express, 162
Albany Plan of Union, 17–19
Albany Public Library, 1
Albany Regency, 150, 153, 162
Albany Rural Cemetery, 95, 111, 160–61
Albany Wide-Awakes, 34, 36, 48
Alfred E. Smith State Office Building, 107, 108
Algonquins, 133, 134
Anthony, Susan B., 37, 38, 39, 40, 41, 42
Anti-Rent Wars, 143–44
Apostate, The, 46, 61
Arbor Hill, 80
Armsby, Dr. James H., 114
Arthur, Chester A., 150, 156–61, **158**
Articles of Union and Confederation, 15
Ash Grove Place, 95, 98
Atlas and Argus, 34, 38, 42, 44, 52, 65
Atzerot, George, 63
aviation, 166–76

Barnes, William F., 82, 115, 162–65
Battery Associates, 57
Bayne Committee, 163
Beal, Moses, 120
beer, 95
Berkshire System, 97
Beverwyck, 77, 84, 142
Block, Adriaen, 6, 7, 8

Bloomer, Amelia, 38
Bogart & Schuyler, 110
Booth, John Wilkes, 43–51, 60–72, **64**
Brant, Joseph, 148
Brant, Molly, 146, 148
British, 14. See also *England; English.*
Brown, Andrew, 28
Buckingham, Rev. Edgar, 66
Burns, Robert (statue of), 114
Burr, Aaron, 20–30, **24,** 151
Burr Conspiracy, 30
Bushnell, Cornelius S., 54, 55, 56

Canada, 6, 12, 133, 148
canal boats, 88, 90
Capital Newspapers, 1
Capitol, 68, 69, 79, 100, 101, 102, **104,** 105, 106, 107, 108, 171
Capitol Hill, 100–109
Carte Figuratif, 5, 6, 8
Cartier, Jacques, 133
Castle Island, 5, 6, 7, 77
Cathedral of the Immaculate Conception, 98
Central Park (New York), 110, 111
Christiaensen, Hendrick, 7
Church, John Barker, 20, 28
Churchill, Winston, 155
circus, 119
City Hall, 79
Civil War, 52–59, 97, 98, 159, 160
Clinton, DeWitt, 28, 76, 153
Clinton, George, 26, 27, 30, 147
"Colonie," The, 85, 141
Congress Hall, 48
Conkling, Roscoe, 159, 160
Connaught Block, 96
Conners, Richard J., 88
Cooper, Charles, 28
Corbett, "Boston," 69
Corlaer, 9
Corning, Edwin, 164, 165
Corning, Erastus, 38, 55, 76, 80, 117, 122
Corning, Erastus Jr., 113

INDEX

Corning, Erastus 2nd, 164
Court of Appeals (building), 107, 108
Crittenden Compromise, 38
Curtiss, Glenn H., 166–76, **169**

D. & H. Railroad, 82, 83, 163; building, 165
Davis, Jefferson, 44, 48, 50
Dawson, George, 32
de Champlain, Samuel, 133–39
Delamater, Cornelius H. (Harry), 53, 54, 56, 58
De Lancey, Gov. James, 16
Delavan House, 40, 41, 47, 50, 82
Dellius, Rev. Godfredius, 92
de Mantet, D'Aillebout, 9
Demis, Dr. D. Joseph, 87
Democratic Party, 27, 37, 38, 40, 162, 164
Dongan Charter, 92, 127
Dongan, Gov. Thomas, 143
Dorpe Beverwyck, 76
Doubleday, Capt. Abner, 51
Douglas, Stephen A., 34, 162
Douglass, Frederick, 41
downtown, 75–83
Draper, Andrew S., 68–69
Dudley Observatory, 49
dueling, 28
Dutch, 5, 6, 75, 134, 137, 139, 140, 141, 142, 146, 151; architecture, 79, 92; church, 93; language, 101, 142. See also *Netherlands*.
Dutch East India Company, 136, 139
Dutch West India Company, 84, 140, 141
Dyer, Rev. David, 66

Edwards, Rev. Jonathan, 22
Eelkens, Jacob, 8
Electoral College, 27
Ellsworth, Elmer, 34, 36, 45–46, **47**, 49, 51
England, 6. See also *British; English*.
Englewood Place, 111
English, 18, 77, 142, 147. See also *British; England*.
epidemics, 80
Ericsson, John, 54–59
Ericsson's Folly, 53
Erie Canal, 88–89, 96, 98, 121, 153
executions, 80, 81, 101
Executive Mansion, 95, 106, 153

Fanciulli, Jerome, 167, 170, 171, 172
farmers' market, 81, 98
Federalist Party, 26, 27, 94
Fenton, Gov. Reuben E., 63, 67
Fiaccabrino, Joseph, 106

Fillmore, Millard, 34, 94
fires, 81, 108
Flexner, James, 146, 147, 148
floods, 7, 8, 14, 80, 81
Ford's Theater, 60, 61, 70
Fort Albany, 77, 100
Fort Crailo, 94, 142
Fort Frederick, 77, 100, 111
Fort Frederick Apartments, 108
Fort Nassau, 5, 6, 7–8, 77
Fort Necessity, 15
Fort Orange, 9, 77, 84, 92, 141, 142
Fort Sumter, 51, 65
Fortune, the, 7
Franklin, Benjamin, 17–19
French, 6, 9, 12, 15, 16, 133, 147
French and Indian War, 12, 93, 129
fur trade, 5–8, 129, 140, 147
Fuyck, The, 77

Galena, 54, 55
Gander Bay, 80
Gansevoort, Leonard, 101
Gansevoort, Peter, 103, 115
Garfield, James A., 156, 159, 160
Garrison, William Lloyd, 42
Germans, 96–97, 142, 163
Glen, John Sander, 12
Glenville, 9
Grant, Ulysses, 60, 159
Grant, Mrs. Ulysses, 60
Great Western Mail, 120
Great Western Turnpike, 121, 122
Greeley, Horace, 32
Green, Rev. Beriah, 41
Griswold, John F., 55, 56, 57
Groesbeck family, 94
"Gut, The," 163

Hackett, William S., 106, 165
"Half-Breeds," 159
Half Moon, 83, 108, 133, 137, 138, 139
Hallenbakes, 94–95
Hamilton, Alexander, 20–30, **24**, 94, 151
Hamilton, Elizabeth Schuyler, 20–21, 28
Hamlin, Mrs. Charles S. See *Pruyn, Huybertie*.
Harmanus Bleeker Hall, 108
Harris, Clara, 61, 62, 69–72. See also *Rathbone, Henry*.
Harris, Ira, 61, 69, 70, 71
Harris, Louise, 70, 71
Harris, W. H., 71
"Helderberg War," 143
Hendrick, King, 15, 16, 147–48
Henry, Joseph, 103, 105; memorial, 79, 105
Herold, Davy, 63, 69

INDEX

Hooker, Philip, 76, 79, 80, 82, 102, 103, 105, 107
Hope Baptist Church, 99
Hudson Flyer, 175
Hudson Fulton Celebration, 166
Hudson, Henry, 6, 7, 102, 133–39
Hudson River, 7, 8, 12–13, 14, 138–39, 166–76
Hudson River Railroad, 50, 51

ice-handlers, 90
immigrants, 75, 92, 95–97, 120, 140, 142
Indians, 6, 7, 9, 12, 14, 127, 134, 137, 141, 143, 145. See also *Algonquins; Iroquois; Mohawks.*
Industrial Revolution, 92
Irish, 90, 96, 142, 147, 156
ironclads, 52–59
Iroquois, 14, 15, 133, 134, 146, 147, 148
Island Creek, 5, 172
Italians, 97

Jackson, Andrew, 152, 154
James, William, 81–82
Jamestown, 5, 6
Jay, John, 26
Jefferson, Thomas, 26, 27, 28, 30, 151
Jerome, Jennie, 155
Jews, 97
Johnson, Andrew, 63, 69
Johnson, Guy, 148
Johnson Hall, 145, 146, 147, 148–49
Johnson, Sir William, 15, 16, 129, 145–49
Jonckers Street. See *State Street.*
Juet, Robert, 138, 139
Jumonville, 15

Kennedy, Joseph P., 106, 107
Kennedy, William, 1
Kent, Chancellor James, 25
Kenwood, 99
King, Henry L., 114–15
King, Rufus H., 114
King's Highway, 126, 128, 129
King William's War, 12
Krank, George, 98

Lafayette, Marquis de, 25, 105
Lafayette Park, 107
Lake Albany, 79
Lake George, 145, 147
Lancaster School, 105
land reforms, 144
Le Moyne de Sainte Helene, 9, 10
Le Moyne d'Iberia, 9
lighting, 82

Limerick, 90
Lincoln, Abraham, 31–36, 37, 38, 43–51, 54, 56, 60–72, **64**, 162;
assassins, 69
Lincoln, Mary Todd, 45, 48, 50, 60, 61, 62, 67, 72
Lindenwald, 154
livestock trade, 117–19
Livingston family, 26, 142
Livingston, Robert, 142
lumber barons, 88–90, 115
Lumber District, 88–91

Mahicans, 141
Manhattan Island, 5
Mauritius River, 7, 140
May, Cornelis Jacobsen, 140, 141
Mayflower, 6
McClellan, George B., 53
McClosky, Bishop John, 98
McDougall, Gen. Alexander, 23
McElroy, Mary Arthur, 160
McElroy, Mrs. Charles E., 71–72
McEwan, James B., 168
McKinney Library, 1
McKown Tavern, 121
Melville, Herman, 103, 105
Memorial Hospital, 99
Merrimac, 52–59
Mohawk and Hudson Railroad, 85, 116, 121, 123, 128
Mohawk Indians, 6, 7, 9, 12, 14, 15, 16, 134, 141, 145, 147
Mohawk River, 8, 9
Molly Maguires, 97
Monitor, 52–59
Morgan, Gov. George, 36, 45, 48, 49, 53, 159
Moses (statue), 114
Mott, Lucretia, 40, 41
Murray, David, 111
Muscovy Company, 135, 136

Netherlands, 5, 6, 8, 136, 140
New Netherland, 140
New Netherland Company, 8
New York Central, 48, 50, 82, 117, 118, 123, 128, 168
New York Times, 58, 168, 172
New York World, 58, 166–76
Normanskill, 7
North Albany, 84–91

O Albany!, 1
O'Connell, Daniel P., 164, 165
Olcott, T. W., 95
Old Dutch Church, 76, 79
Olmstead, Frederick, 110
Onrust, 8

INDEX

Orson, 7, 8
Osborne, Danvers, 16

Paine, Lewis, 62–63
Palmer, Erastus Dow, 114
Parker, Amasa, 38
Pasture, The, 92–93
Pastures, The. See *Schuyler Mansion.*
Patroon (place), 84, 140–44
patroonship, 85
Pearl St., 81
Perry, Eli, 67, 68
Phoenix Club, 86
Pine Bush, 125–30
Pine Hills, 116, 124
Pinkster, 101–02
plagues, 80. See also *epidemics.*
politicians, 95
Port of Albany, 8, 92, 167
Prince Maurice, 5, 7, 141
Princeton, the, 56
Pruyn, Huybertie, 86

Quackenbush House, 79

railroads, 122–23, 127. See also individual lines.
Rathbone, Henry, 51, 61, 62, 68, 70–72
Rathbone, Jared, 61
Rensselaer Iron Works, 59
Rensselaer Lake, 128
Rensselaerswyck, 84, 141
Republican Party, 31, 32, 159, 162, 163
Reynolds, Cuyler, 120
Reynolds, Marcus T., 76, 82–83, 86, 163
Rhind, J. Massey, 115
Richardson, H. H., 107, 108
Roseberry, C. R., x

Sacandaga Reservoir, 7
St. Peter's Church, 76
Sawyer, "Poppy," 98–99
Schenectady Massacre, 9–13
Schenectady stockade, **11**
Schermerhorn, Simon, 10–12
Schmidt, Theobald. See *Smith, Theobald.*
Schuyler, Catherine, 21, 94
Schuyler Mansion, 22, 23, 94, 98
Schuyler, Pieter, 12, 143
Schuyler, Philip, 20–30, 85, 93, 94, 95, 97
Schuyler, Samuel, 97
Schuyler Towing Line, 98
Schuylerville, 9
Seward, Frederick, 31, 34, 36, 51, 63, 67
Seward, William H., 31–36, **33**, 51, 56, 62, 63, 67, 95

Shakers, 125, 129
shipping industry, 81
Shirley, Gov. William, 15
Six Mile Water Works, 128, 129
slavery, 37–42, 101
Smith, Alfred E., 106–07, 164. See also *Alfred E. Smith Building.*
Smith, Gerrit, 40, 41
Smith, Captain John, 134, 135, 137
Smith, Commodore Joseph, 56
Smith, Theobald, 95–96
South End, 92–99
Spain, 1, 5, 6, 136
Spoils System, 150, 156, 159
Sprague, William, 66
Stadt Huys, 14, 16, 79, 100, 102
stagecoaches, 120–21
"Stalwarts," 159
Standard Building, 107
Stanton, Edwin M., 52, 60, 63, 67
Stanton, Elizabeth Cady, 38, 40, 41
Stanwix Hall, 43, 50, 51, 82
State St. *(Jonckers St.),* 76, 77, 80
statues, 114
stockyards, 117–19
stove industry, 97
streams, 80, 95
street names, 77, 103, 106, 127
strikes, 97, 118, 165
Stone, Lucy, 38
Stuyvesant, Peter, 84, 142
South End, 92–99, 167
SUNYA, 120

Talmadge, Lieut., 10
Tammany Hall, 151, 153
Tayler, Judge John, 28
Ten Eyck Hotel, 170, 172
Ten Eyck, Jacob, 167, 170, 172
Thacher, George H., 37–42, **39**, 49
Thacher, John Boyd II, 76, 176
Thomas, Rev. Jacob, 66
Thurlow Terrace (neighborhood), 115
Tiger, The, 7, 8
Times Union, 1
Troup, Robert, 22, 23

Union College, 37, 61, 157
union of colonies (idea), 13, 17–19
Union Station, 82

Valentine, 7
Van Buren, Martin, 150–55, **152,** 162
Van Buren, "Prince John," 151, 154, 155
Van Curler, Arendt, 9, 142
Van Rensselaer family, 84, 85, 84–91, 117, 141
Van Rensselaer Island, 5, 97, 167
Van Rensselaer, Jeremiah, 84, 93

INDEX 197

Van Rensselaer, Kiliaen, 84, 141, 142
Van Rensselaer Manor, 84, 85, 86, 88, 142, 143
Van Rensselaer, Philip Schuyler, 102
Van Rensselaer, Stephen III, 85, **87**, 121, 122, 143
Van Rensselaer, Stephen IV (the Young Patroon), 85, 128, 143, 144
Van Rensselaer, William Patterson, 143
Vaux, Calvert, 110
Verreberg, 128
Virginia, 6
Vrooman, Adam, 10

Walloons, 140, 141
Warraghiyagey, 145
Washington, George, 15, 22, 25, 26, 93
Washington Park, 110–13, **112**
waterfront, 82
water supply, 80
Watson, Elkanah, 75, 76, **78,** 79
Weed, Thurlow, 31, 32, 34, **35,** 36, 115, 122, 123, 162, 163

Weehawken, 21, **24,** 28
Weisenberg, Catherine, 148
Welles, Gideon, 55, 56
West Albany, 116–19
West Albany car shops, 49, 117
Westerlo Island, 5
Westland Hills, 111, 122
whaling, 93
Whig Party, 31
Wide-Awakes. See *Albany Wide-Awakes.*
Widow Truax Tavern, 129
Willemstadt, 77, 142
Willett, Col. Marinus, 115
Willett St., 115
Williams College, 86
Winslow, John F., 55, 56, 57
Wright, Wilbur, 166
women's suffrage, 37–42, 164
Worden, John L., 58, 59

Yates, Abraham, 95

Zouave Cadets, 34, 36, 49

Book Design: Diana S. Waite, Mount Ida Press
Cover Design: C. Timm Associates
Typography: Williams Press
Printing: Crest Litho
Photo Credits: Page 11, *The Story of the Schenectady Massacre,* Schenectady County Historical Society, 1940. Page 33 and page 35, the New York State Archives. Page 169, The J. Lansing Collection, courtesy of C. R. Roseberry. Back cover, Nicholas Argyros. All other photographs from the collection of the McKinney Library, Albany Institute of History and Art.